GNU M4 Reference Manual

A catalogue record for this book is available from the Hong Kong Public Libraries.

Published in Hong Kong by Samurai Media Limited.

Email: info@samuraimedia.org

ISBN 978-988-8381-50-0

Table of Contents

GNU `m4` is an implementation of the traditional UNIX macro processor. It is mostly SVR4 compatible, although it has some extensions (for example, handling more than 9 positional parameters to macros). `m4` also has builtin functions for including files, running shell commands, doing arithmetic, etc. Autoconf needs GNU `m4` for generating `configure` scripts, but not for running them.

GNU `m4` was originally written by René Seindal, with subsequent changes by François Pinard and other volunteers on the Internet. All names and email addresses can be found in the files `m4-1.4.17/AUTHORS` and `m4-1.4.17/THANKS` from the GNU M4 distribution.

This is release 1.4.17. It is now considered stable: future releases in the 1.4.x series are only meant to fix bugs, increase speed, or improve documentation. However...

An experimental feature, which would improve `m4` usefulness, allows for changing the syntax for what is a *word* in `m4`. You should use:

```
./configure --enable-changeword
```

if you want this feature compiled in. The current implementation slows down `m4` considerably and is hardly acceptable. In the future, `m4` 2.0 will come with a different set of new features that provide similar capabilities, but without the inefficiencies, so changeword will go away and *you should not count on it*.

1 Introduction and preliminaries

This first chapter explains what GNU m4 is, where m4 comes from, how to read and use this documentation, how to call the m4 program, and how to report bugs about it. It concludes by giving tips for reading the remainder of the manual.

The following chapters then detail all the features of the m4 language.

1.1 Introduction to m4

m4 is a macro processor, in the sense that it copies its input to the output, expanding macros as it goes. Macros are either builtin or user-defined, and can take any number of arguments. Besides just doing macro expansion, m4 has builtin functions for including named files, running shell commands, doing integer arithmetic, manipulating text in various ways, performing recursion, etc.... m4 can be used either as a front-end to a compiler, or as a macro processor in its own right.

The m4 macro processor is widely available on all UNIXes, and has been standardized by POSIX. Usually, only a small percentage of users are aware of its existence. However, those who find it often become committed users. The popularity of GNU Autoconf, which requires GNU m4 for *generating* configure scripts, is an incentive for many to install it, while these people will not themselves program in m4. GNU m4 is mostly compatible with the System V, Release 4 version, except for some minor differences. See Chapter 16 [Compatibility], page 109, for more details.

Some people find m4 to be fairly addictive. They first use m4 for simple problems, then take bigger and bigger challenges, learning how to write complex sets of m4 macros along the way. Once really addicted, users pursue writing of sophisticated m4 applications even to solve simple problems, devoting more time debugging their m4 scripts than doing real work. Beware that m4 may be dangerous for the health of compulsive programmers.

1.2 Historical references

Macro languages were invented early in the history of computing. In the 1950s Alan Perlis suggested that the macro language be independent of the language being processed. Techniques such as conditional and recursive macros, and using macros to define other macros, were described by Doug McIlroy of Bell Labs in "Macro Instruction Extensions of Compiler Languages", *Communications of the ACM* 3, 4 (1960), 214–20, http://dx.doi.org/10.1145/367177.367223.

An important precursor of m4 was GPM; see C. Strachey, "A general purpose macrogenerator", *Computer Journal* 8, 3 (1965), 225–41, http://dx.doi.org/10.1093/comjnl/8.3.225. GPM is also succinctly described in David Gries's book *Compiler Construction for Digital Computers*, Wiley (1971). Strachey was a brilliant programmer: GPM fit into 250 machine instructions!

Inspired by GPM while visiting Strachey's Lab in 1968, McIlroy wrote a model preprocessor in that fit into a page of Snobol 3 code, and McIlroy and Robert Morris developed a series of further models at Bell Labs. Andrew D. Hall followed up with M6, a general purpose macro processor used to port the Fortran source code of the Altran computer algebra system; see Hall's "The M6 Macro Processor", Computing Science Technical Report

#2, Bell Labs (1972), `http://cm.bell-labs.com/cm/cs/cstr/2.pdf`. M6's source code consisted of about 600 Fortran statements. Its name was the first of the `m4` line.

The Brian Kernighan and P.J. Plauger book *Software Tools*, Addison-Wesley (1976), describes and implements a Unix macro-processor language, which inspired Dennis Ritchie to write `m3`, a macro processor for the AP-3 minicomputer.

Kernighan and Ritchie then joined forces to develop the original `m4`, described in "The M4 Macro Processor", Bell Laboratories (1977), `http://wolfram.schneider.org/bsd/7thEdManVol2/m4/m4.pdf`. It had only 21 builtin macros.

While `GPM` was more *pure*, `m4` is meant to deal with the true intricacies of real life: macros can be recognized without being pre-announced, skipping whitespace or end-of-lines is easier, more constructs are builtin instead of derived, etc.

Originally, the Kernighan and Plauger macro-processor, and then `m3`, formed the engine for the Rational FORTRAN preprocessor, that is, the `Ratfor` equivalent of `cpp`. Later, `m4` was used as a front-end for `Ratfor`, `C` and `Cobol`.

René Seindal released his implementation of `m4`, GNU `m4`, in 1990, with the aim of removing the artificial limitations in many of the traditional `m4` implementations, such as maximum line length, macro size, or number of macros.

The late Professor A. Dain Samples described and implemented a further evolution in the form of M5: "User's Guide to the M5 Macro Language: 2nd edition", Electronic Announcement on comp.compilers newsgroup (1992).

François Pinard took over maintenance of GNU `m4` in 1992, until 1994 when he released GNU `m4` 1.4, which was the stable release for 10 years. It was at this time that GNU Autoconf decided to require GNU `m4` as its underlying engine, since all other implementations of `m4` had too many limitations.

More recently, in 2004, Paul Eggert released 1.4.1 and 1.4.2 which addressed some long standing bugs in the venerable 1.4 release. Then in 2005, Gary V. Vaughan collected together the many patches to GNU `m4` 1.4 that were floating around the net and released 1.4.3 and 1.4.4. And in 2006, Eric Blake joined the team and prepared patches for the release of 1.4.5, 1.4.6, 1.4.7, and 1.4.8. More bug fixes were incorporated in 2007, with releases 1.4.9 and 1.4.10. Eric continued with some portability fixes for 1.4.11 and 1.4.12 in 2008, 1.4.13 in 2009, 1.4.14 and 1.4.15 in 2010, and 1.4.16 in 2011.

Meanwhile, development has continued on new features for `m4`, such as dynamic module loading and additional builtins. When complete, GNU `m4` 2.0 will start a new series of releases.

1.3 Problems and bugs

If you have problems with GNU M4 or think you've found a bug, please report it. Before reporting a bug, make sure you've actually found a real bug. Carefully reread the documentation and see if it really says you can do what you're trying to do. If it's not clear whether you should be able to do something or not, report that too; it's a bug in the documentation!

Before reporting a bug or trying to fix it yourself, try to isolate it to the smallest possible input file that reproduces the problem. Then send us the input file and the exact results `m4` gave you. Also say what you expected to occur; this will help us decide whether the problem was really in the documentation.

Once you've got a precise problem, send e-mail to bug-m4@gnu.org. Please include the version number of m4 you are using. You can get this information with the command *m4 --version*. Also provide details about the platform you are executing on.

Non-bug suggestions are always welcome as well. If you have questions about things that are unclear in the documentation or are just obscure features, please report them too.

1.4 Using this manual

This manual contains a number of examples of m4 input and output, and a simple notation is used to distinguish input, output and error messages from m4. Examples are set out from the normal text, and shown in a fixed width font, like this

```
This is an example of an example!
```

To distinguish input from output, all output from m4 is prefixed by the string '⇒', and all error messages by the string ' error '. When showing how command line options affect matters, the command line is shown with a prompt '$ *like this*', otherwise, you can assume that a simple m4 invocation will work. Thus:

```
$ command line to invoke m4
Example of input line
⇒Output line from m4
error  and an error message
```

The sequence '^D' in an example indicates the end of the input file. The sequence 'NL' refers to the newline character. The majority of these examples are self-contained, and you can run them with similar results by invoking *m4 -d*. In fact, the testsuite that is bundled in the GNU M4 package consists of the examples in this document! Some of the examples assume that your current directory is located where you unpacked the installation, so if you plan on following along, you may find it helpful to do this now:

```
$ cd m4-1.4.17
```

As each of the predefined macros in m4 is described, a prototype call of the macro will be shown, giving descriptive names to the arguments, e.g.,

example (*string*, [*count* = '1'], [*argument*]...)   [Composite]
> This is a sample prototype. There is not really a macro named example, but this documents that if there were, it would be a Composite macro, rather than a Builtin. It requires at least one argument, *string*. Remember that in m4, there must not be a space between the macro name and the opening parenthesis, unless it was intended to call the macro without any arguments. The brackets around *count* and *argument* show that these arguments are optional. If *count* is omitted, the macro behaves as if count were '1', whereas if *argument* is omitted, the macro behaves as if it were the empty string. A blank argument is not the same as an omitted argument. For example, 'example('a')', 'example('a','1')', and 'example('a','1',)' would behave identically with *count* set to '1'; while 'example('a',)' and 'example('a','')' would explicitly pass the empty string for *count*. The ellipses ('...') show that the macro processes additional arguments after *argument*, rather than ignoring them.

All macro arguments in m4 are strings, but some are given special interpretation, e.g., as numbers, file names, regular expressions, etc. The documentation for each macro will state how the parameters are interpreted, and what happens if the argument cannot be parsed according to the desired interpretation. Unless specified otherwise, a parameter specified to be a number is parsed as a decimal, even if the argument has leading zeros; and parsing the empty string as a number results in 0 rather than an error, although a warning will be issued.

This document consistently writes and uses *builtin*, without a hyphen, as if it were an English word. This is how the `builtin` primitive is spelled within `m4`.

2 Invoking m4

The format of the m4 command is:

        m4 [option...] [file...]

All options begin with '-', or if long option names are used, with '--'. A long option name need not be written completely, any unambiguous prefix is sufficient. POSIX requires m4 to recognize arguments intermixed with files, even when POSIXLY_CORRECT is set in the environment. Most options take effect at startup regardless of their position, but some are documented below as taking effect after any files that occurred earlier in the command line. The argument -- is a marker to denote the end of options.

With short options, options that do not take arguments may be combined into a single command line argument with subsequent options, options with mandatory arguments may be provided either as a single command line argument or as two arguments, and options with optional arguments must be provided as a single argument. In other words, m4 -QPDfoo -d a -df is equivalent to m4 -Q -P -D foo -d -df -- ./a, although the latter form is considered canonical.

With long options, options with mandatory arguments may be provided with an equal sign ('=') in a single argument, or as two arguments, and options with optional arguments must be provided as a single argument. In other words, m4 --def foo --debug a is equivalent to m4 --define=foo --debug= -- ./a, although the latter form is considered canonical (not to mention more robust, in case a future version of m4 introduces an option named --default).

m4 understands the following options, grouped by functionality.

2.1 Command line options for operation modes

Several options control the overall operation of m4:

--help   Print a help summary on standard output, then immediately exit m4 without reading any input files or performing any other actions.

--version
            Print the version number of the program on standard output, then immediately exit m4 without reading any input files or performing any other actions.

-E
--fatal-warnings
            Controls the effect of warnings. If unspecified, then execution continues and exit status is unaffected when a warning is printed. If specified exactly once, warnings become fatal; when one is issued, execution continues, but the exit status will be non-zero. If specified multiple times, then execution halts with non-zero status the first time a warning is issued. The introduction of behavior levels is new to M4 1.4.9; for behavior consistent with earlier versions, you should specify -E twice.

-i
--interactive
-e   Makes this invocation of m4 interactive. This means that all output will be unbuffered, and interrupts will be ignored. The spelling -e exists for compati-

bility with other m4 implementations, and issues a warning because it may be withdrawn in a future version of GNU M4.

-P

--prefix-builtins

Internally modify *all* builtin macro names so they all start with the prefix 'm4_'. For example, using this option, one should write 'm4_define' instead of 'define', and 'm4___file__' instead of '__file__'. This option has no effect if -R is also specified.

-Q

--quiet

--silent   Suppress warnings, such as missing or superfluous arguments in macro calls, or treating the empty string as zero.

--warn-macro-sequence[=*regexp*]

Issue a warning if the regular expression *regexp* has a non-empty match in any macro definition (either by **define** or **pushdef**). Empty matches are ignored; therefore, supplying the empty string as *regexp* disables any warning. If the optional *regexp* is not supplied, then the default regular expression is '\$\({[^}]*}\|[0-9][0-9]+\)' (a literal '$' followed by multiple digits or by an open brace), since these sequences will change semantics in the default operation of GNU M4 2.0 (due to a change in how more than 9 arguments in a macro definition will be handled, see Section 5.2 [Arguments], page 26). Providing an alternate regular expression can provide a useful reverse lookup feature of finding where a macro is defined to have a given definition.

-W *regexp*

--word-regexp=*regexp*

Use *regexp* as an alternative syntax for macro names. This experimental option will not be present in all GNU m4 implementations (see Section 8.4 [Changeword], page 67).

2.2 Command line options for preprocessor features

Several options allow m4 to behave more like a preprocessor. Macro definitions and deletions can be made on the command line, the search path can be altered, and the output file can track where the input came from. These features occur with the following options:

-D *name*[=*value*]

--define=*name*[=*value*]

This enters *name* into the symbol table. If '=*value*' is missing, the value is taken to be the empty string. The *value* can be any string, and the macro can be defined to take arguments, just as if it was defined from within the input. This option may be given more than once; order with respect to file names is significant, and redefining the same *name* loses the previous value.

`-I `*`directory`*
`--include=`*`directory`*

> Make `m4` search *directory* for included files that are not found in the current working directory. See Section 9.2 [Search Path], page 74, for more details. This option may be given more than once.

`-s`

`--synclines`

> Generate synchronization lines, for use by the C preprocessor or other similar tools. Order is significant with respect to file names. This option is useful, for example, when `m4` is used as a front end to a compiler. Source file name and line number information is conveyed by directives of the form '`#line `*`linenum`*` "`*`file`*`"`', which are inserted as needed into the middle of the output. Such directives mean that the following line originated or was expanded from the contents of input file *file* at line *linenum*. The '`"`*`file`*`"`' part is often omitted when the file name did not change from the previous directive.
>
> Synchronization directives are always given on complete lines by themselves. When a synchronization discrepancy occurs in the middle of an output line, the associated synchronization directive is delayed until the next newline that does not occur in the middle of a quoted string or comment.

```
define('twoline', '1
2')
⇒#line 2 "stdin"
⇒
changecom('/*', '*/')
⇒
define('comment', '/*1
2*/')
⇒#line 5
⇒
dnl no line
hello
⇒#line 7
⇒hello
twoline
⇒1
⇒#line 8
⇒2
comment
⇒/*1
⇒2*/
one comment 'two
three'
⇒#line 10
⇒one /*1
⇒2*/ two
⇒three
```

```
          goodbye
          ⇒#line 12
          ⇒goodbye
```

`-U` *name*

`--undefine=`*name*

> This deletes any predefined meaning *name* might have. Obviously, only prede-
> fined macros can be deleted in this way. This option may be given more than
> once; undefining a *name* that does not have a definition is silently ignored.
> Order is significant with respect to file names.

2.3 Command line options for limits control

There are some limits within `m4` that can be tuned. For compatibility, `m4` also accepts
some options that control limits in other implementations, but which are automatically
unbounded (limited only by your hardware and operating system constraints) in GNU `m4`.

`-g`

`--gnu`
> Enable all the extensions in this implementation. In this release of M4, this op-
> tion is always on by default; it is currently only useful when overriding a prior
> use of `--traditional`. However, having GNU behavior as default makes it
> impossible to write a strictly POSIX-compliant client that avoids all incompat-
> ible GNU M4 extensions, since such a client would have to use the non-POSIX
> command-line option to force full POSIX behavior. Thus, a future version of
> M4 will be changed to implicitly use the option `--traditional` if the environ-
> ment variable `POSIXLY_CORRECT` is set. Projects that intentionally use GNU
> extensions should consider using `--gnu` to state their intentions, so that the
> project will not mysteriously break if the user upgrades to a newer M4 and has
> `POSIXLY_CORRECT` set in their environment.

`-G`

`--traditional`
> Suppress all the extensions made in this implementation, compared to the Sys-
> tem V version. See Chapter 16 [Compatibility], page 109, for a list of these.

`-H` *num*

`--hashsize=`*num*
> Make the internal hash table for symbol lookup be *num* entries big. For better
> performance, the number should be prime, but this is not checked. The default
> is 509 entries. It should not be necessary to increase this value, unless you
> define an excessive number of macros.

`-L` *num*

`--nesting-limit=`*num*
> Artificially limit the nesting of macro calls to *num* levels, stopping program
> execution if this limit is ever exceeded. When not specified, nesting defaults
> to unlimited on platforms that can detect stack overflow, and to 1024 levels
> otherwise. A value of zero means unlimited; but then heavily nested code could
> potentially cause a stack overflow.

The precise effect of this option is more correctly associated with textual nesting than dynamic recursion. It has been useful when some complex m4 input was generated by mechanical means, and also in diagnosing recursive algorithms that do not scale well. Most users never need to change this option from its default.

This option does *not* have the ability to break endless rescanning loops, since these do not necessarily consume much memory or stack space. Through clever usage of rescanning loops, one can request complex, time-consuming computations from m4 with useful results. Putting limitations in this area would break m4 power. There are many pathological cases: 'define('a', 'a')a' is only the simplest example (but see Chapter 16 [Compatibility], page 109). Expecting GNU m4 to detect these would be a little like expecting a compiler system to detect and diagnose endless loops: it is a quite *hard* problem in general, if not undecidable!

-B *num*
-S *num*
-T *num*   These options are present for compatibility with System V m4, but do nothing in this implementation. They may disappear in future releases, and issue a warning to that effect.

-N *num*
--diversions=*num*
              These options are present only for compatibility with previous versions of GNU m4, and were controlling the number of possible diversions which could be used at the same time. They do nothing, because there is no fixed limit anymore. They may disappear in future releases, and issue a warning to that effect.

2.4 Command line options for frozen state

GNU m4 comes with a feature of freezing internal state (see Chapter 15 [Frozen files], page 105). This can be used to speed up m4 execution when reusing a common initialization script.

-F *file*
--freeze-state=*file*
              Once execution is finished, write out the frozen state on the specified *file*. It is conventional, but not required, for *file* to end in '.m4f'.

-R *file*
--reload-state=*file*
              Before execution starts, recover the internal state from the specified frozen *file*. The options -D, -U, and -t take effect after state is reloaded, but before the input files are read.

2.5 Command line options for debugging

Finally, there are several options for aiding in debugging m4 scripts.

-d[*flags*]
--debug[=*flags*]

> Set the debug-level according to the flags *flags*. The debug-level controls the
> format and amount of information presented by the debugging functions. See
> Section 7.3 [Debug Levels], page 58, for more details on the format and meaning
> of *flags*. If omitted, *flags* defaults to 'aeq'.

--debugfile[=*file*]
-o *file*
--error-output=*file*

> Redirect dumpdef output, debug messages, and trace output to the named *file*.
> Warnings, error messages, and errprint output are still printed to standard
> error. If these options are not used, or if *file* is unspecified (only possible for
> --debugfile), debug output goes to standard error; if *file* is the empty string,
> debug output is discarded. See Section 7.4 [Debug Output], page 60, for more
> details. The option --debugfile may be given more than once, and order is
> significant with respect to file names. The spellings -o and --error-output
> are misleading and inconsistent with other GNU tools; for now they are silently
> accepted as synonyms of --debugfile and only recognized once, but in a future
> version of M4, using them will cause a warning to be issued.

-l *num*
--arglength=*num*

> Restrict the size of the output generated by macro tracing to *num* characters
> per trace line. If unspecified or zero, output is unlimited. See Section 7.3
> [Debug Levels], page 58, for more details.

-t *name*
--trace=*name*

> This enables tracing for the macro *name*, at any point where it is defined. *name*
> need not be defined when this option is given. This option may be given more
> than once, and order is significant with respect to file names. See Section 7.2
> [Trace], page 55, for more details.

2.6 Specifying input files on the command line

The remaining arguments on the command line are taken to be input file names. If no
names are present, standard input is read. A file name of - is taken to mean standard
input. It is conventional, but not required, for input files to end in '.m4'.

The input files are read in the sequence given. Standard input can be read more than
once, so the file name - may appear multiple times on the command line; this makes a
difference when input is from a terminal or other special file type. It is an error if an input
file ends in the middle of argument collection, a comment, or a quoted string.

The options --define (-D), --undefine (-U), --synclines (-s), and --trace (-t) only
take effect after processing input from any file names that occur earlier on the command
line. For example, assume the file foo contains:

```
$ cat foo
bar
```

The text 'bar' can then be redefined over multiple uses of foo:

```
$ m4 -Dbar=hello foo -Dbar=world foo
⇒hello
⇒world
```

If none of the input files invoked m4exit (see Section 14.3 [M4exit], page 103), the exit status of m4 will be 0 for success, 1 for general failure (such as problems with reading an input file), and 63 for version mismatch (see Section 15.1 [Using frozen files], page 105).

If you need to read a file whose name starts with a -, you can specify it as './-file', or use -- to mark the end of options.

3 Lexical and syntactic conventions

As m4 reads its input, it separates it into *tokens*. A token is either a name, a quoted string, or any single character, that is not a part of either a name or a string. Input to m4 can also contain comments. GNU m4 does not yet understand multibyte locales; all operations are byte-oriented rather than character-oriented (although if your locale uses a single byte encoding, such as ISO-8859-1, you will not notice a difference). However, m4 is eight-bit clean, so you can use non-ASCII characters in quoted strings (see Section 8.2 [Changequote], page 62), comments (see Section 8.3 [Changecom], page 65), and macro names (see Section 5.7 [Indir], page 34), with the exception of the NUL character (the zero byte ''\0'').

3.1 Macro names

A name is any sequence of letters, digits, and the character '_' (underscore), where the first character is not a digit. m4 will use the longest such sequence found in the input. If a name has a macro definition, it will be subject to macro expansion (see Chapter 4 [Macros], page 19). Names are case-sensitive.

Examples of legal names are: 'foo', '_tmp', and 'name01'.

3.2 Quoting input to m4

A quoted string is a sequence of characters surrounded by quote strings, defaulting to '' and '', where the nested begin and end quotes within the string are balanced. The value of a string token is the text, with one level of quotes stripped off. Thus

```
''
⇒
```

is the empty string, and double-quoting turns into single-quoting.

```
''quoted''
⇒'quoted'
```

The quote characters can be changed at any time, using the builtin macro changequote. See Section 8.2 [Changequote], page 62, for more information.

3.3 Comments in m4 input

Comments in m4 are normally delimited by the characters '#' and newline. All characters between the comment delimiters are ignored, but the entire comment (including the delimiters) is passed through to the output—comments are *not* discarded by m4.

Comments cannot be nested, so the first newline after a '#' ends the comment. The commenting effect of the begin-comment string can be inhibited by quoting it.

```
$ m4
'quoted text' # 'commented text'
⇒quoted text # 'commented text'
'quoting inhibits' '#' 'comments'
⇒quoting inhibits # comments
```

The comment delimiters can be changed to any string at any time, using the builtin macro changecom. See Section 8.3 [Changecom], page 65, for more information.

3.4 Other kinds of input tokens

Any character, that is neither a part of a name, nor of a quoted string, nor a comment, is a token by itself. When not in the context of macro expansion, all of these tokens are just copied to output. However, during macro expansion, whitespace characters (space, tab, newline, formfeed, carriage return, vertical tab), parentheses ('(' and ')'), comma (','), and dollar ('$') have additional roles, explained later.

3.5 How m4 copies input to output

As m4 reads the input token by token, it will copy each token directly to the output immediately.

The exception is when it finds a word with a macro definition. In that case m4 will calculate the macro's expansion, possibly reading more input to get the arguments. It then inserts the expansion in front of the remaining input. In other words, the resulting text from a macro call will be read and parsed into tokens again.

m4 expands a macro as soon as possible. If it finds a macro call when collecting the arguments to another, it will expand the second call first. This process continues until there are no more macro calls to expand and all the input has been consumed.

For a running example, examine how m4 handles this input:

```
format('Result is %d', eval('2**15'))
```

First, m4 sees that the token 'format' is a macro name, so it collects the tokens '(', ''Result is %d'', ',', and ' ', before encountering another potential macro. Sure enough, 'eval' is a macro name, so the nested argument collection picks up '(', ''2**15'', and ')', invoking the eval macro with the lone argument of '2**15'. The expansion of 'eval(2**15)' is '32768', which is then rescanned as the five tokens '3', '2', '7', '6', and '8'; and combined with the next ')', the format macro now has all its arguments, as if the user had typed:

```
format('Result is %d', 32768)
```

The format macro expands to 'Result is 32768', and we have another round of scanning for the tokens 'Result', ' ', 'is', ' ', '3', '2', '7', '6', and '8'. None of these are macros, so the final output is

```
⇒Result is 32768
```

As a more complicated example, we will contrast an actual code example from the Gnulib project[1], showing both a buggy approach and the desired results. The user desires to output a shell assignment statement that takes its argument and turns it into a shell variable by converting it to uppercase and prepending a prefix. The original attempt looks like this:

```
changequote([,])dnl
define([gl_STRING_MODULE_INDICATOR],
  [
    dnl comment
    GNULIB_]translit([$1],[a-z],[A-Z])[=1
  ])dnl
  gl_STRING_MODULE_INDICATOR([strcase])
```

---

[1] Derived from a patch in http://lists.gnu.org/archive/html/bug-gnulib/2007-01/msg00389.html, and a followup patch in http://lists.gnu.org/archive/html/bug-gnulib/2007-02/msg00000.html

⇒
⇒   GNULIB_strcase=1
⇒

Oops – the argument did not get capitalized. And although the manual is not able to easily show it, both lines that appear empty actually contain two trailing spaces. By stepping through the parse, it is easy to see what happened. First, m4 sees the token 'changequote', which it recognizes as a macro, followed by '(', '[', ',', ']', and ')' to form the argument list. The macro expands to the empty string, but changes the quoting characters to something more useful for generating shell code (unbalanced '`' and '`' appear all the time in shell scripts, but unbalanced '[]' tend to be rare). Also in the first line, m4 sees the token 'dnl', which it recognizes as a builtin macro that consumes the rest of the line, resulting in no output for that line.

The second line starts a macro definition. m4 sees the token 'define', which it recognizes as a macro, followed by a '(', '[gl_STRING_MODULE_INDICATOR]', and ','. Because an unquoted comma was encountered, the first argument is known to be the expansion of the single-quoted string token, or 'gl_STRING_MODULE_INDICATOR'. Next, m4 sees 'NL', ' ', and ' ', but this whitespace is discarded as part of argument collection. Then comes a rather lengthy single-quoted string token, '[NL   dnl commentNL   GNULIB_]'. This is followed by the token 'translit', which m4 recognizes as a macro name, so a nested macro expansion has started.

The arguments to the translit are found by the tokens '(', '[$1]', ',', '[a-z]', ',', '[A-Z]', and finally ')'. All three string arguments are expanded (or in other words, the quotes are stripped), and since neither '$' nor '1' need capitalization, the result of the macro is '$1'. This expansion is rescanned, resulting in the two literal characters '$' and '1'.

Scanning of the outer macro resumes, and picks up with '[=1NL   ]', and finally ')'. The collected pieces of expanded text are concatenated, with the end result that the macro 'gl_STRING_MODULE_INDICATOR' is now defined to be the sequence 'NL   dnl commentNL GNULIB_$1=1NL   '. Once again, 'dnl' is recognized and avoids a newline in the output.

The final line is then parsed, beginning with ' ' and ' ' that are output literally. Then 'gl_STRING_MODULE_INDICATOR' is recognized as a macro name, with an argument list of '(', '[strcase]', and ')'. Since the definition of the macro contains the sequence '$1', that sequence is replaced with the argument 'strcase' prior to starting the rescan. The rescan sees 'NL' and four spaces, which are output literally, then 'dnl', which discards the text ' commentNL'. Next comes four more spaces, also output literally, and the token 'GNULIB_strcase', which resulted from the earlier parameter substitution. Since that is not a macro name, it is output literally, followed by the literal tokens '=', '1', 'NL', and two more spaces. Finally, the original 'NL' seen after the macro invocation is scanned and output literally.

Now for a corrected approach. This rearranges the use of newlines and whitespace so that less whitespace is output (which, although harmless to shell scripts, can be visually unappealing), and fixes the quoting issues so that the capitalization occurs when the macro 'gl_STRING_MODULE_INDICATOR' is invoked, rather then when it is defined. It also adds another layer of quoting to the first argument of translit, to ensure that the output will be rescanned as a string rather than a potential uppercase macro name needing further expansion.

```
changequote([,])dnl
define([gl_STRING_MODULE_INDICATOR],
  [dnl comment
  GNULIB_[]translit([[$1]], [a-z], [A-Z])=1dnl
])dnl
  gl_STRING_MODULE_INDICATOR([strcase])
⇒     GNULIB_STRCASE=1
```

The parsing of the first line is unchanged. The second line sees the name of the macro to define, then sees the discarded 'NL' and two spaces, as before. But this time, the next token is '[dnl commentNL GNULIB_[]translit([[$1]], [a-z], [A-Z])=1dnlNL]', which includes nested quotes, followed by ')' to end the macro definition and 'dnl' to skip the newline. No early expansion of translit occurs, so the entire string becomes the definition of the macro.

The final line is then parsed, beginning with two spaces that are output literally, and an invocation of gl_STRING_MODULE_INDICATOR with the argument 'strcase'. Again, the '$1' in the macro definition is substituted prior to rescanning. Rescanning first encounters 'dnl', and discards ' commentNL'. Then two spaces are output literally. Next comes the token 'GNULIB_', but that is not a macro, so it is output literally. The token '[]' is an empty string, so it does not affect output. Then the token 'translit' is encountered.

This time, the arguments to translit are parsed as '(', '[[strcase]]', ',', ' ', '[a-z]', ',', ' ', '[A-Z]', and ')'. The two spaces are discarded, and the translit results in the desired result '[STRCASE]'. This is rescanned, but since it is a string, the quotes are stripped and the only output is a literal 'STRCASE'. Then the scanner sees '=' and '1', which are output literally, followed by 'dnl' which discards the rest of the definition of gl_STRING_MODULE_INDICATOR. The newline at the end of output is the literal 'NL' that appeared after the invocation of the macro.

The order in which m4 expands the macros can be further explored using the trace facilities of GNU m4 (see Section 7.2 [Trace], page 55).

4 How to invoke macros

This chapter covers macro invocation, macro arguments and how macro expansion is treated.

4.1 Macro invocation

Macro invocations has one of the forms

```
name
```

which is a macro invocation without any arguments, or

```
name(arg1, arg2, ..., argn)
```

which is a macro invocation with n arguments. Macros can have any number of arguments. All arguments are strings, but different macros might interpret the arguments in different ways.

The opening parenthesis *must* follow the *name* directly, with no spaces in between. If it does not, the macro is called with no arguments at all.

For a macro call to have no arguments, the parentheses *must* be left out. The macro call

```
name()
```

is a macro call with one argument, which is the empty string, not a call with no arguments.

4.2 Preventing macro invocation

An innovation of the m4 language, compared to some of its predecessors (like Strachey's GPM, for example), is the ability to recognize macro calls without resorting to any special, prefixed invocation character. While generally useful, this feature might sometimes be the source of spurious, unwanted macro calls. So, GNU m4 offers several mechanisms or techniques for inhibiting the recognition of names as macro calls.

First of all, many builtin macros cannot meaningfully be called without arguments. As a GNU extension, for any of these macros, whenever an opening parenthesis does not immediately follow their name, the builtin macro call is not triggered. This solves the most usual cases, like for 'include' or 'eval'. Later in this document, the sentence "This macro is recognized only with parameters" refers to this specific provision of GNU M4, also known as a blind builtin macro. For the builtins defined by POSIX that bear this disclaimer, POSIX specifically states that invoking those builtins without arguments is unspecified, because many other implementations simply invoke the builtin as though it were given one empty argument instead.

```
$ m4
eval
⇒eval
eval('1')
⇒1
```

There is also a command line option (--prefix-builtins, or -P, see Section 2.1 [Invoking m4], page 7) that renames all builtin macros with a prefix of 'm4_' at startup. The option has no effect whatsoever on user defined macros. For example, with this option, one has to write m4_dnl and even m4_m4exit. It also has no effect on whether a macro requires parameters.

```
$ m4 -P
eval
⇒eval
eval('1')
⇒eval(1)
m4_eval
⇒m4_eval
m4_eval('1')
⇒1
```

Another alternative is to redefine problematic macros to a name less likely to cause conflicts, using Chapter 5 [Definitions], page 25.

If your version of GNU m4 has the **changeword** feature compiled in, it offers far more flexibility in specifying the syntax of macro names, both builtin or user-defined. See Section 8.4 [Changeword], page 67, for more information on this experimental feature.

Of course, the simplest way to prevent a name from being interpreted as a call to an existing macro is to quote it. The remainder of this section studies a little more deeply how quoting affects macro invocation, and how quoting can be used to inhibit macro invocation.

Even if quoting is usually done over the whole macro name, it can also be done over only a few characters of this name (provided, of course, that the unquoted portions are not also a macro). It is also possible to quote the empty string, but this works only *inside* the name. For example:

```
'divert'
⇒divert
'd'ivert
⇒divert
di'ver't
⇒divert
div''ert
⇒divert
```

all yield the string 'divert'. While in both:

```
''divert
⇒
divert''
⇒
```

the **divert** builtin macro will be called, which expands to the empty string.

The output of macro evaluations is always rescanned. In the following example, the input 'x''y' yields the string 'bCD', exactly as if m4 has been given 'substr(ab''cde, '1', '3')' as input:

```
define('cde', 'CDE')
⇒
define('x', 'substr(ab')
⇒
define('y', 'cde, '1', '3')')
⇒
x''y
```

```
⇒bCD
```

Unquoted strings on either side of a quoted string are subject to being recognized as macro names. In the following example, quoting the empty string allows for the second `macro` to be recognized as such:

```
define('macro', 'm')
⇒
macro('m')macro
⇒mmacro
macro('m')''macro
⇒mm
```

Quoting may prevent recognizing as a macro name the concatenation of a macro expansion with the surrounding characters. In this example:

```
define('macro', 'di$1')
⇒
macro('v')'ert'
⇒divert
macro('v')ert
⇒
```

the input will produce the string 'divert'. When the quotes were removed, the `divert` builtin was called instead.

4.3 Macro arguments

When a name is seen, and it has a macro definition, it will be expanded as a macro.

If the name is followed by an opening parenthesis, the arguments will be collected before the macro is called. If too few arguments are supplied, the missing arguments are taken to be the empty string. However, some builtins are documented to behave differently for a missing optional argument than for an explicit empty string. If there are too many arguments, the excess arguments are ignored. Unquoted leading whitespace is stripped off all arguments, but whitespace generated by a macro expansion or occurring after a macro that expanded to an empty string remains intact. Whitespace includes space, tab, newline, carriage return, vertical tab, and formfeed.

```
define('macro', '$1')
⇒
macro( unquoted leading space lost)
⇒unquoted leading space lost
macro(' quoted leading space kept')
⇒ quoted leading space kept
macro(
  divert 'unquoted space kept after expansion')
⇒ unquoted space kept after expansion
macro(macro('
')'whitespace from expansion kept')
⇒
⇒whitespace from expansion kept
macro('unquoted trailing whitespace kept'
```

```
)
⇒unquoted trailing whitespace kept
⇒
```

Normally m4 will issue warnings if a builtin macro is called with an inappropriate number of arguments, but it can be suppressed with the --quiet command line option (or --silent, or -Q, see Section 2.1 [Invoking m4], page 7). For user defined macros, there is no check of the number of arguments given.

```
$ m4
index('abc')
error m4:stdin:1: Warning: too few arguments to builtin 'index'
⇒0
index('abc',)
⇒0
index('abc', 'b', 'ignored')
error m4:stdin:3: Warning: excess arguments to builtin 'index' ignored
⇒1
$ m4 -Q
index('abc')
⇒0
index('abc',)
⇒0
index('abc', 'b', 'ignored')
⇒1
```

Macros are expanded normally during argument collection, and whatever commas, quotes and parentheses that might show up in the resulting expanded text will serve to define the arguments as well. Thus, if *foo* expands to ', b, c', the macro call

```
bar(a foo, d)
```

is a macro call with four arguments, which are 'a ', 'b', 'c' and 'd'. To understand why the first argument contains whitespace, remember that unquoted leading whitespace is never part of an argument, but trailing whitespace always is.

It is possible for a macro's definition to change during argument collection, in which case the expansion uses the definition that was in effect at the time the opening '(' was seen.

```
define('f', '1')
⇒
f(define('f', '2'))
⇒1
f
⇒2
```

It is an error if the end of file occurs while collecting arguments.

```
hello world
⇒hello world
define(
^D
error m4:stdin:2: ERROR: end of file in argument list
```

4.4 On Quoting Arguments to macros

Each argument has unquoted leading whitespace removed. Within each argument, all unquoted parentheses must match. For example, if *foo* is a macro,

```
foo(() ('(') '(')
```

is a macro call, with one argument, whose value is '() (() ('. Commas separate arguments,
except when they occur inside quotes, comments, or unquoted parentheses. See Section 5.3
[Pseudo Arguments], page 27, for examples.

It is common practice to quote all arguments to macros, unless you are sure you want
the arguments expanded. Thus, in the above example with the parentheses, the 'right' way
to do it is like this:

```
foo('() (() (')
```

It is, however, in certain cases necessary (because nested expansion must occur to create
the arguments for the outer macro) or convenient (because it uses fewer characters) to leave
out quotes for some arguments, and there is nothing wrong in doing it. It just makes life a
bit harder, if you are not careful to follow a consistent quoting style. For consistency, this
manual follows the rule of thumb that each layer of parentheses introduces another layer
of single quoting, except when showing the consequences of quoting rules. This is done
even when the quoted string cannot be a macro, such as with integers when you have not
changed the syntax via **changeword** (see Section 8.4 [Changeword], page 67).

The quoting rule of thumb of one level of quoting per parentheses has a nice property:
when a macro name appears inside parentheses, you can determine when it will be expanded.
If it is not quoted, it will be expanded prior to the outer macro, so that its expansion becomes
the argument. If it is single-quoted, it will be expanded after the outer macro. And if it is
double-quoted, it will be used as literal text instead of a macro name.

```
define('active', 'ACT, IVE')
⇒
define('show', '$1 $1')
⇒
show(active)
⇒ACT ACT
show('active')
⇒ACT, IVE ACT, IVE
show(''active'')
⇒active active
```

4.5 Macro expansion

When the arguments, if any, to a macro call have been collected, the macro is expanded, and
the expansion text is pushed back onto the input (unquoted), and reread. The expansion
text from one macro call might therefore result in more macros being called, if the calls are
included, completely or partially, in the first macro calls' expansion.

Taking a very simple example, if *foo* expands to '`bar`', and *bar* expands to '`Hello`', the
input

```
$ m4 -Dbar=Hello -Dfoo=bar
foo
```

⇒`Hello`

will expand first to '`bar`', and when this is reread and expanded, into '`Hello`'.

5 How to define new macros

Macros can be defined, redefined and deleted in several different ways. Also, it is possible to redefine a macro without losing a previous value, and bring back the original value at a later time.

5.1 Defining a macro

The normal way to define or redefine macros is to use the builtin `define`:

define (*name*, [*expansion*])   [Builtin]

> Defines *name* to expand to *expansion*. If *expansion* is not given, it is taken to be empty.
>
> The expansion of `define` is void. The macro `define` is recognized only with parameters.

The following example defines the macro *foo* to expand to the text 'Hello World.'.

```
define('foo', 'Hello world.')
⇒
foo
⇒Hello world.
```

The empty line in the output is there because the newline is not a part of the macro definition, and it is consequently copied to the output. This can be avoided by use of the macro `dnl`. See Section 8.1 [Dnl], page 61, for details.

The first argument to `define` should be quoted; otherwise, if the macro is already defined, you will be defining a different macro. This example shows the problems with underquoting, since we did not want to redefine `one`:

```
define(foo, one)
⇒
define(foo, two)
⇒
one
⇒two
```

GNU `m4` normally replaces only the *topmost* definition of a macro if it has several definitions from `pushdef` (see Section 5.6 [Pushdef], page 33). Some other implementations of `m4` replace all definitions of a macro with `define`. See Section 16.2 [Incompatibilities], page 110, for more details.

As a GNU extension, the first argument to `define` does not have to be a simple word. It can be any text string, even the empty string. A macro with a non-standard name cannot be invoked in the normal way, as the name is not recognized. It can only be referenced by the builtins `indir` (see Section 5.7 [Indir], page 34) and `defn` (see Section 5.5 [Defn], page 31).

Arrays and associative arrays can be simulated by using non-standard macro names.

array (*index*)   [Composite]
array_set (*index*, [*value*])   [Composite]

> Provide access to entries within an array. `array` reads the entry at location *index*, and `array_set` assigns *value* to location *index*.

```
define('array', 'defn(format(''array[%d]'', '$1'))')
⇒
define('array_set', 'define(format(''array[%d]'', '$1'), '$2')')
⇒
array_set('4', 'array element no. 4')
⇒
array_set('17', 'array element no. 17')
⇒
array('4')
⇒array element no. 4
array(eval('10 + 7'))
⇒array element no. 17
```

Change the '%d' to '%s' and it is an associative array.

5.2 Arguments to macros

Macros can have arguments. The nth argument is denoted by $n in the expansion text, and is replaced by the nth actual argument, when the macro is expanded. Replacement of arguments happens before rescanning, regardless of how many nesting levels of quoting appear in the expansion. Here is an example of a macro with two arguments.

exch (*arg1*, *arg2*)   [Composite]
  Expands to *arg2* followed by *arg1*, effectively exchanging their order.

```
define('exch', '$2, $1')
⇒
exch('arg1', 'arg2')
⇒arg2, arg1
```

This can be used, for example, if you like the arguments to **define** to be reversed.

```
define('exch', '$2, $1')
⇒
define(exch(''expansion text'', ''macro''))
⇒
macro
⇒expansion text
```

See Section 4.4 [Quoting Arguments], page 23, for an explanation of the double quotes. (You should try and improve this example so that clients of **exch** do not have to double quote; or see Section 17.1 [Answers], page 115).

As a special case, the zeroth argument, $0, is always the name of the macro being expanded.

```
define('test', ''Macro name: $0'')
⇒
test
⇒Macro name: test
```

If you want quoted text to appear as part of the expansion text, remember that quotes can be nested in quoted strings. Thus, in

```
define('foo', 'This is macro 'foo'.')
⇒
foo
⇒This is macro foo.
```

The 'foo' in the expansion text is *not* expanded, since it is a quoted string, and not a name.

GNU `m4` allows the number following the '$' to consist of one or more digits, allowing macros to have any number of arguments. The extension of accepting multiple digits is incompatible with POSIX, and is different than traditional implementations of `m4`, which only recognize one digit. Therefore, future versions of GNU M4 will phase out this feature. To portably access beyond the ninth argument, you can use the `argn` macro documented later (see Section 6.3 [Shift], page 41).

POSIX also states that '$' followed immediately by '{' in a macro definition is implementation-defined. This version of M4 passes the literal characters '${' through unchanged, but M4 2.0 will implement an optional feature similar to `sh`, where '${11}' expands to the eleventh argument, to replace the current recognition of '$11'. Meanwhile, if you want to guarantee that you will get a literal '${' in output when expanding a macro, even when you upgrade to M4 2.0, you can use nested quoting to your advantage:

```
define('foo', 'single quoted $''{1} output')
⇒
define('bar', ''double quoted $''{2} output'')
⇒
foo('a', 'b')
⇒single quoted ${1} output
bar('a', 'b')
⇒double quoted ${2} output
```

To help you detect places in your M4 input files that might change in behavior due to the changed behavior of M4 2.0, you can use the `--warn-macro-sequence` command-line option (see Section 2.1 [Invoking m4], page 7) with the default regular expression. This will add a warning any time a macro definition includes '$' followed by multiple digits, or by '{'. The warning is not enabled by default, because it triggers a number of warnings in Autoconf 2.61 (and Autoconf uses -E to treat warnings as errors), and because it will still be possible to restore older behavior in M4 2.0.

```
$ m4 --warn-macro-sequence
define('foo', '$001 ${1} $1')
error m4:stdin:1: Warning: definition of 'foo' contains sequence '$001'
error m4:stdin:1: Warning: definition of 'foo' contains sequence '${1}'
⇒
foo('bar')
⇒bar ${1} bar
```

5.3 Special arguments to macros

There is a special notation for the number of actual arguments supplied, and for all the actual arguments.

The number of actual arguments in a macro call is denoted by `$#` in the expansion text.

nargs (...)   [Composite]
     Expands to a count of the number of arguments supplied.

```
define('nargs', '$#')
⇒
nargs
⇒0
nargs()
⇒1
nargs('arg1', 'arg2', 'arg3')
⇒3
nargs('commas can be quoted, like this')
⇒1
nargs(arg1#inside comments, commas do not separate arguments
still arg1)
⇒1
nargs((unquoted parentheses, like this, group arguments))
⇒1
```

Remember that '#' defaults to the comment character; if you forget quotes to inhibit the comment behavior, your macro definition may not end where you expected.

```
dnl Attempt to define a macro to just '$#'
define(underquoted, $#)
oops)
⇒
underquoted
⇒0)
⇒oops
```

The notation $* can be used in the expansion text to denote all the actual arguments, unquoted, with commas in between. For example

```
define('echo', '$*')
⇒
echo(arg1,    arg2, arg3 , arg4)
⇒arg1,arg2,arg3 ,arg4
```

Often each argument should be quoted, and the notation $@ handles that. It is just like $*, except that it quotes each argument. A simple example of that is:

```
define('echo', '$@')
⇒
echo(arg1,    arg2, arg3 , arg4)
⇒arg1,arg2,arg3 ,arg4
```

Where did the quotes go? Of course, they were eaten, when the expanded text were reread by m4. To show the difference, try

```
define('echo1', '$*')
⇒
define('echo2', '$@')
⇒
define('foo', 'This is macro 'foo'.')
```

```
⇒
echo1(foo)
⇒This is macro This is macro foo..
echo1(`foo')
⇒This is macro foo.
echo2(foo)
⇒This is macro foo.
echo2(`foo')
⇒foo
```

See Section 7.2 [Trace], page 55, if you do not understand this. As another example of the
difference, remember that comments encountered in arguments are passed untouched to the
macro, and that quoting disables comments.

```
define(`echo1', `$*')
⇒
define(`echo2', `$@')
⇒
define(`foo', `bar')
⇒
echo1(#foo'foo
foo)
⇒#foo'foo
⇒bar
echo2(#foo'foo
foo)
⇒#foobar
⇒bar'
```

A '$' sign in the expansion text, that is not followed by anything m4 understands, is
simply copied to the macro expansion, as any other text is.

```
define(`foo', `$$$ hello $$$')
⇒
foo
⇒$$$ hello $$$
```

If you want a macro to expand to something like '$12', the judicious use of nested quoting
can put a safe character between the $ and the next character, relying on the rescanning to
remove the nested quote. This will prevent m4 from interpreting the $ sign as a reference
to an argument.

```
define(`foo', `no nested quote: $1')
⇒
foo(`arg')
⇒no nested quote: arg
define(`foo', `nested quote around $: `$'1')
⇒
foo(`arg')
⇒nested quote around $: $1
define(`foo', `nested empty quote after $: $`'1')
```

```
⇒
foo('arg')
⇒nested empty quote after $: $1
define('foo', 'nested quote around next character: $'1'')
⇒
foo('arg')
⇒nested quote around next character: $1
define('foo', 'nested quote around both: '$1'')
⇒
foo('arg')
⇒nested quote around both: arg
```

5.4 Deleting a macro

A macro definition can be removed with `undefine`:

undefine (*name*...)   [Builtin]

>   For each argument, remove the macro *name*. The macro names must necessarily be
>   quoted, since they will be expanded otherwise.

>   The expansion of `undefine` is void. The macro `undefine` is recognized only with
>   parameters.

```
foo bar blah
⇒foo bar blah
define('foo', 'some')define('bar', 'other')define('blah', 'text')
⇒
foo bar blah
⇒some other text
undefine('foo')
⇒
foo bar blah
⇒foo other text
undefine('bar', 'blah')
⇒
foo bar blah
⇒foo bar blah
```

>   Undefining a macro inside that macro's expansion is safe; the macro still expands to the
>   definition that was in effect at the '('.

```
define('f', ''$0':$1')
⇒
f(f(f(undefine('f')'hello world')))
⇒f:f:f:hello world
f('bye')
⇒f(bye)
```

It is not an error for *name* to have no macro definition. In that case, `undefine` does
nothing.

5.5 Renaming macros

It is possible to rename an already defined macro. To do this, you need the builtin **defn**:

defn (*name...*)   [Builtin]

> Expands to the *quoted definition* of each *name*. If an argument is not a defined macro, the expansion for that argument is empty.
>
> If *name* is a user-defined macro, the quoted definition is simply the quoted expansion text. If, instead, there is only one *name* and it is a builtin, the expansion is a special token, which points to the builtin's internal definition. This token is only meaningful as the second argument to **define** (and **pushdef**), and is silently converted to an empty string in most other contexts. Combining a builtin with anything else is not supported; a warning is issued and the builtin is omitted from the final expansion.
>
> The macro **defn** is recognized only with parameters.

Its normal use is best understood through an example, which shows how to rename **undefine** to **zap**:

```
define('zap', defn('undefine'))
⇒
zap('undefine')
⇒
undefine('zap')
⇒undefine(zap)
```

In this way, **defn** can be used to copy macro definitions, and also definitions of builtin macros. Even if the original macro is removed, the other name can still be used to access the definition.

The fact that macro definitions can be transferred also explains why you should use **$0**, rather than retyping a macro's name in its definition:

```
define('foo', 'This is '$0'')
⇒
define('bar', defn('foo'))
⇒
bar
⇒This is bar
```

Macros used as string variables should be referred through **defn**, to avoid unwanted expansion of the text:

```
define('string', 'The macro dnl is very useful
')
⇒
string
⇒The macro
defn('string')
⇒The macro dnl is very useful
⇒
```

However, it is important to remember that **m4** rescanning is purely textual. If an unbalanced end-quote string occurs in a macro definition, the rescan will see that embedded

quote as the termination of the quoted string, and the remainder of the macro's definition
will be rescanned unquoted. Thus it is a good idea to avoid unbalanced end-quotes in macro
definitions or arguments to macros.

```
define('foo', a'a)
⇒
define('a', 'A')
⇒
define('echo', '$@')
⇒
foo
⇒A'A
defn('foo')
⇒aA'
echo(foo)
⇒AA'
```

On the other hand, it is possible to exploit the fact that **defn** can concatenate multiple
macros prior to the rescanning phase, in order to join the definitions of macros that, in
isolation, have unbalanced quotes. This is particularly useful when one has used several
macros to accumulate text that M4 should rescan as a whole. In the example below, note
how the use of **defn** on l in isolation opens a string, which is not closed until the next line;
but used on l and r together results in nested quoting.

```
define('l', '<[>')define('r', '<]>')
⇒
changequote('[', ']')
⇒
defn([l])defn([r])
])
⇒<[>]defn([r])
⇒)
defn([l], [r])
⇒<[>][<]>
```

Using **defn** to generate special tokens for builtin macros outside of expected contexts
can sometimes trigger warnings. But most of the time, such tokens are silently converted
to the empty string.

```
$ m4 -d
defn('defn')
⇒
define(defn('divnum'), 'cannot redefine a builtin token')
error m4:stdin:2: Warning: define: invalid macro name ignored
⇒
divnum
⇒0
len(defn('divnum'))
⇒0
```

Also note that **defn** with multiple arguments can only join text macros, not builtins,
although a future version of GNU M4 may lift this restriction.

```
$ m4 -d
define(`a', `A')define(`AA', `b')
⇒
traceon(`defn', `define')
⇒
defn(`a', `divnum', `a')
    error  m4:stdin:3: Warning: cannot concatenate builtin `divnum'
    error  m4trace: -1- defn(`a', `divnum', `a') -> ``A'`A''
⇒AA
define(`mydivnum', defn(`divnum', `divnum'))mydivnum
    error  m4:stdin:4: Warning: cannot concatenate builtin `divnum'
    error  m4:stdin:4: Warning: cannot concatenate builtin `divnum'
    error  m4trace: -2- defn(`divnum', `divnum')
    error  m4trace: -1- define(`mydivnum', `')
⇒
traceoff(`defn', `define')
⇒
```

5.6 Temporarily redefining macros

It is possible to redefine a macro temporarily, reverting to the previous definition at a later time. This is done with the builtins pushdef and popdef:

pushdef (*name*, [*expansion*])   [Builtin]
popdef (*name*...)   [Builtin]

>   Analogous to define and undefine.

>   These macros work in a stack-like fashion. A macro is temporarily redefined with pushdef, which replaces an existing definition of *name*, while saving the previous definition, before the new one is installed. If there is no previous definition, pushdef behaves exactly like define.

>   If a macro has several definitions (of which only one is accessible), the topmost definition can be removed with popdef. If there is no previous definition, popdef behaves like undefine.

>   The expansion of both pushdef and popdef is void. The macros pushdef and popdef are recognized only with parameters.

```
define(`foo', `Expansion one.')
⇒
foo
⇒Expansion one.
pushdef(`foo', `Expansion two.')
⇒
foo
⇒Expansion two.
pushdef(`foo', `Expansion three.')
⇒
pushdef(`foo', `Expansion four.')
⇒
```

```
popdef('foo')
⇒
foo
⇒Expansion three.
popdef('foo', 'foo')
⇒
foo
⇒Expansion one.
popdef('foo')
⇒
foo
⇒foo
```

If a macro with several definitions is redefined with **define**, the topmost definition is *replaced* with the new definition. If it is removed with **undefine**, *all* the definitions are removed, and not only the topmost one. However, POSIX allows other implementations that treat **define** as replacing an entire stack of definitions with a single new definition, so to be portable to other implementations, it may be worth explicitly using **popdef** and **pushdef** rather than relying on the GNU behavior of **define**.

```
define('foo', 'Expansion one.')
⇒
foo
⇒Expansion one.
pushdef('foo', 'Expansion two.')
⇒
foo
⇒Expansion two.
define('foo', 'Second expansion two.')
⇒
foo
⇒Second expansion two.
undefine('foo')
⇒
foo
⇒foo
```

Local variables within macros are made with **pushdef** and **popdef**. At the start of the macro a new definition is pushed, within the macro it is manipulated and at the end it is popped, revealing the former definition.

It is possible to temporarily redefine a builtin with **pushdef** and **defn**.

5.7 Indirect call of macros

Any macro can be called indirectly with **indir**:

indir (*name*, [*args*...])   [Builtin]
    Results in a call to the macro *name*, which is passed the rest of the arguments *args*. If *name* is not defined, an error message is printed, and the expansion is void.

    The macro **indir** is recognized only with parameters.

This can be used to call macros with computed or "invalid" names (`define` allows such names to be defined):

```
define('$$internal$macro', 'Internal macro (name '$0')')
⇒
$$internal$macro
⇒$$internal$macro
indir('$$internal$macro')
⇒Internal macro (name $$internal$macro)
```

The point is, here, that larger macro packages can have private macros defined, that will not be called by accident. They can *only* be called through the builtin `indir`.

One other point to observe is that argument collection occurs before `indir` invokes *name*, so if argument collection changes the value of *name*, that will be reflected in the final expansion. This is different than the behavior when invoking macros directly, where the definition that was in effect before argument collection is used.

```
$ m4 -d
define('f', '1')
⇒
f(define('f', '2'))
⇒1
indir('f', define('f', '3'))
⇒3
indir('f', undefine('f'))
error m4:stdin:4: undefined macro 'f'
⇒
```

When handed the result of `defn` (see Section 5.5 [Defn], page 31) as one of its arguments, `indir` defers to the invoked *name* for whether a token representing a builtin is recognized or flattened to the empty string.

```
$ m4 -d
indir(defn('defn'), 'divnum')
error m4:stdin:1: Warning: indir: invalid macro name ignored
⇒
indir('define', defn('defn'), 'divnum')
error m4:stdin:2: Warning: define: invalid macro name ignored
⇒
indir('define', 'foo', defn('divnum'))
⇒
foo
⇒0
indir('divert', defn('foo'))
error m4:stdin:5: empty string treated as 0 in builtin 'divert'
⇒
```

5.8 Indirect call of builtins

Builtin macros can be called indirectly with `builtin`:

builtin (*name*, [*args*...])   [Builtin]
>   Results in a call to the builtin *name*, which is passed the rest of the arguments *args*.
>   If *name* does not name a builtin, an error message is printed, and the expansion is
>   void.
>
>   The macro builtin is recognized only with parameters.

This can be used even if *name* has been given another definition that has covered the
original, or been undefined so that no macro maps to the builtin.

```
pushdef('define', 'hidden')
⇒
undefine('undefine')
⇒
define('foo', 'bar')
⇒hidden
foo
⇒foo
builtin('define', 'foo', defn('divnum'))
⇒
foo
⇒0
builtin('define', 'foo', 'BAR')
⇒
foo
⇒BAR
undefine('foo')
⇒undefine(foo)
foo
⇒BAR
builtin('undefine', 'foo')
⇒
foo
⇒foo
```

The *name* argument only matches the original name of the builtin, even when the --
prefix-builtins option (or -P, see Section 2.1 [Invoking m4], page 7) is in effect. This is
different from indir, which only tracks current macro names.

```
$ m4 -P
m4_builtin('divnum')
⇒0
m4_builtin('m4_divnum')
error m4:stdin:2: undefined builtin 'm4_divnum'
⇒
m4_indir('divnum')
error m4:stdin:3: undefined macro 'divnum'
⇒
m4_indir('m4_divnum')
⇒0
```

Note that `indir` and `builtin` can be used to invoke builtins without arguments, even when they normally require parameters to be recognized; but it will provoke a warning, and result in a void expansion.

```
builtin
⇒builtin
builtin()
error m4:stdin:2: undefined builtin ‘’
⇒
builtin(‘builtin’)
error m4:stdin:3: Warning: too few arguments to builtin ‘builtin’
⇒
builtin(‘builtin’,)
error m4:stdin:4: undefined builtin ‘’
⇒
builtin(‘builtin’, ‘‘’
’)
error m4:stdin:5: undefined builtin ‘‘’
error ’
⇒
indir(‘index’)
error m4:stdin:7: Warning: too few arguments to builtin ‘index’
⇒
```

6 Conditionals, loops, and recursion

Macros, expanding to plain text, perhaps with arguments, are not quite enough. We would like to have macros expand to different things, based on decisions taken at run-time. For that, we need some kind of conditionals. Also, we would like to have some kind of loop construct, so we could do something a number of times, or while some condition is true.

6.1 Testing if a macro is defined

There are two different builtin conditionals in m4. The first is ifdef:

ifdef (*name, string-1,* [*string-2*])   [Builtin]

> If *name* is defined as a macro, ifdef expands to *string-1*, otherwise to *string-2*. If *string-2* is omitted, it is taken to be the empty string (according to the normal rules).
>
> The macro ifdef is recognized only with parameters.
>
> ```
> ifdef(`foo', ``foo' is defined', ``foo' is not defined')
> ⇒foo is not defined
> define(`foo', `')
> ⇒
> ifdef(`foo', ``foo' is defined', ``foo' is not defined')
> ⇒foo is defined
> ifdef(`no_such_macro', `yes', `no', `extra argument')
> error m4:stdin:4: Warning: excess arguments to builtin `ifdef' ignored
> ⇒no
> ```

6.2 If-else construct, or multibranch

The other conditional, ifelse, is much more powerful. It can be used as a way to introduce a long comment, as an if-else construct, or as a multibranch, depending on the number of arguments supplied:

ifelse (*comment*)   [Builtin]
ifelse (*string-1, string-2, equal,* [*not-equal*])   [Builtin]
ifelse (*string-1, string-2, equal-1, string-3, string-4, equal-2,*   [Builtin]
     ..., [*not-equal*])

> Used with only one argument, the ifelse simply discards it and produces no output.
>
> If called with three or four arguments, ifelse expands into *equal*, if *string-1* and *string-2* are equal (character for character), otherwise it expands to *not-equal*. A final fifth argument is ignored, after triggering a warning.
>
> If called with six or more arguments, and *string-1* and *string-2* are equal, ifelse expands into *equal-1*, otherwise the first three arguments are discarded and the processing starts again.
>
> The macro ifelse is recognized only with parameters.

Using only one argument is a common m4 idiom for introducing a block comment, as an alternative to repeatedly using dnl. This special usage is recognized by GNU m4, so that in this case, the warning about missing arguments is never triggered.

```
ifelse('some comments')
⇒
ifelse('foo', 'bar')
error m4:stdin:2: Warning: too few arguments to builtin 'ifelse'
⇒
```

Using three or four arguments provides decision points.

```
ifelse('foo', 'bar', 'true')
⇒
ifelse('foo', 'foo', 'true')
⇒true
define('foo', 'bar')
⇒
ifelse(foo, 'bar', 'true', 'false')
⇒true
ifelse(foo, 'foo', 'true', 'false')
⇒false
```

Notice how the first argument was used unquoted; it is common to compare the expansion of a macro with a string. With this macro, you can now reproduce the behavior of blind builtins, where the macro is recognized only with arguments.

```
define('foo', 'ifelse('$#', '0', ''$0'', 'arguments:$#')')
⇒
foo
⇒foo
foo()
⇒arguments:1
foo('a', 'b', 'c')
⇒arguments:3
```

For an example of a way to make defining blind macros easier, see Section 6.7 [Composition], page 51.

The macro `ifelse` can take more than four arguments. If given more than four arguments, `ifelse` works like a `case` or `switch` statement in traditional programming languages. If *string-1* and *string-2* are equal, `ifelse` expands into *equal-1*, otherwise the procedure is repeated with the first three arguments discarded. This calls for an example:

```
ifelse('foo', 'bar', 'third', 'gnu', 'gnats')
error m4:stdin:1: Warning: excess arguments to builtin 'ifelse' ignored
⇒gnu
ifelse('foo', 'bar', 'third', 'gnu', 'gnats', 'sixth')
⇒
ifelse('foo', 'bar', 'third', 'gnu', 'gnats', 'sixth', 'seventh')
⇒seventh
ifelse('foo', 'bar', '3', 'gnu', 'gnats', '6', '7', '8')
error m4:stdin:4: Warning: excess arguments to builtin 'ifelse' ignored
⇒7
```

Naturally, the normal case will be slightly more advanced than these examples. A common use of `ifelse` is in macros implementing loops of various kinds.

6.3 Recursion in m4

There is no direct support for loops in m4, but macros can be recursive. There is no limit on the number of recursion levels, other than those enforced by your hardware and operating system.

Loops can be programmed using recursion and the conditionals described previously.

There is a builtin macro, shift, which can, among other things, be used for iterating through the actual arguments to a macro:

shift (*arg1*, ...)   [Builtin]

    Takes any number of arguments, and expands to all its arguments except *arg1*, separated by commas, with each argument quoted.

    The macro shift is recognized only with parameters.

```
shift
⇒shift
shift('bar')
⇒
shift('foo', 'bar', 'baz')
⇒bar,baz
```

An example of the use of shift is this macro:

reverse (...)   [Composite]

    Takes any number of arguments, and reverses their order.

    It is implemented as:

```
define('reverse', 'ifelse('$#', '0', , '$#', '1', ''$1'',
                          'reverse(shift($@)), '$1'')')
⇒
reverse
⇒
reverse('foo')
⇒foo
reverse('foo', 'bar', 'gnats', 'and gnus')
⇒and gnus, gnats, bar, foo
```

While not a very interesting macro, it does show how simple loops can be made with shift, ifelse and recursion. It also shows that shift is usually used with '$@'. Another example of this is an implementation of a short-circuiting conditional operator.

cond (*test-1*, *string-1*, *equal-1*, [*test-2*], [*string-2*], [*equal-2*],   [Composite]
    ..., [*not-equal*])

    Similar to ifelse, where an equal comparison between the first two strings results in the third, otherwise the first three arguments are discarded and the process repeats. The difference is that each *test-<n>* is expanded only when it is encountered. This means that every third argument to cond is normally given one more level of quoting than the corresponding argument to ifelse.

Here is the implementation of cond, along with a demonstration of how it can short-circuit the side effects in side. Notice how all the unquoted side effects happen regardless of how many comparisons are made with ifelse, compared with only the relevant effects with cond.

```
define('cond',
'ifelse('$#', '1', '$1',
        'ifelse($1, '$2', '$3',
                '$0(shift(shift(shift($@))))')')')')dnl
define('side', 'define('counter', incr(counter))$1')dnl
define('example1',
'define('counter', '0')dnl
ifelse(side('$1'), 'yes', 'one comparison: ',
       side('$1'), 'no', 'two comparisons: ',
       side('$1'), 'maybe', 'three comparisons: ',
       'side('default answer: ')')counter')dnl
define('example2',
'define('counter', '0')dnl
cond('side('$1')', 'yes', 'one comparison: ',
     'side('$1')', 'no', 'two comparisons: ',
     'side('$1')', 'maybe', 'three comparisons: ',
     'side('default answer: ')')counter')dnl
example1('yes')
⇒one comparison: 3
example1('no')
⇒two comparisons: 3
example1('maybe')
⇒three comparisons: 3
example1('feeling rather indecisive today')
⇒default answer: 4
example2('yes')
⇒one comparison: 1
example2('no')
⇒two comparisons: 2
example2('maybe')
⇒three comparisons: 3
example2('feeling rather indecisive today')
⇒default answer: 4
```

Another common task that requires iteration is joining a list of arguments into a single string.

join ([*separator*], [*args...*])   [Composite]
joinall ([*separator*], [*args...*])   [Composite]
    Generate a single-quoted string, consisting of each *arg* separated by *separator*. While joinall always outputs a *separator* between arguments, join avoids the *separator* for an empty *arg*.

Here are some examples of its usage, based on the implementation m4-1.4.17/examples/join.m4 distributed in this package:

```
$ m4 -I examples
include('join.m4')
⇒
join,join('-'),join('-', ''),join('-', '', '')
⇒,,,
joinall,joinall('-'),joinall('-', ''),joinall('-', '', '')
⇒,,,-
join('-', '1')
⇒1
join('-', '1', '2', '3')
⇒1-2-3
join('', '1', '2', '3')
⇒123
join('-', '', '1', '', '', '2', '')
⇒1-2
joinall('-', '', '1', '', '', '2', '')
⇒-1---2-
join(',', '1', '2', '3')
⇒1,2,3
define('nargs', '$#')dnl
nargs(join(',', '1', '2', '3'))
⇒1
```

Examining the implementation shows some interesting points about several m4 programming idioms.

```
$ m4 -I examples
undivert('join.m4')dnl
⇒divert('-1')
⇒# join(sep, args) - join each non-empty ARG into a single
⇒# string, with each element separated by SEP
⇒define('join',
⇒'ifelse('$#', '2', ''$2'',
⇒  'ifelse('$2', '', '', ''$2'_')$0('$1', shift(shift($@)))')')
⇒define('_join',
⇒'ifelse('$#$2', '2', '',
⇒  'ifelse('$2', '', '', ''$1$2'')$0('$1', shift(shift($@)))')')
⇒# joinall(sep, args) - join each ARG, including empty ones,
⇒# into a single string, with each element separated by SEP
⇒define('joinall', ''$2'_$0('$1', shift($@))')
⇒define('_joinall',
⇒'ifelse('$#', '2', '', ''$1$3'$0('$1', shift(shift($@)))')')
⇒divert''dnl
```

First, notice that this implementation creates helper macros _join and _joinall. This division of labor makes it easier to output the correct number of *separator* instances: join and joinall are responsible for the first argument, without a separator, while _join and _joinall are responsible for all remaining arguments, always outputting a separator when outputting an argument.

Next, observe how join decides to iterate to itself, because the first *arg* was empty, or to output the argument and swap over to _join. If the argument is non-empty, then the nested ifelse results in an unquoted '_', which is concatenated with the '$0' to form the next macro name to invoke. The joinall implementation is simpler since it does not have to suppress empty *arg*; it always executes once then defers to _joinall.

Another important idiom is the idea that *separator* is reused for each iteration. Each iteration has one less argument, but rather than discarding '$1' by iterating with $0(shift($@)), the macro discards '$2' by using $0('$1', shift(shift($@))).

Next, notice that it is possible to compare more than one condition in a single ifelse test. The test of '$#$2' against '2' allows _join to iterate for two separate reasons—either there are still more than two arguments, or there are exactly two arguments but the last argument is not empty.

Finally, notice that these macros require exactly two arguments to terminate recursion, but that they still correctly result in empty output when given no *args* (i.e., zero or one macro argument). On the first pass when there are too few arguments, the shift results in no output, but leaves an empty string to serve as the required second argument for the second pass. Put another way, ''$1', shift($@)' is not the same as '$@', since only the former guarantees at least two arguments.

Sometimes, a recursive algorithm requires adding quotes to each element, or treating multiple arguments as a single element:

quote (...)   [Composite]
dquote (...)   [Composite]
dquote_elt (...)   [Composite]

> Takes any number of arguments, and adds quoting. With quote, only one level of quoting is added, effectively removing whitespace after commas and turning multiple arguments into a single string. With dquote, two levels of quoting are added, one around each element, and one around the list. And with dquote_elt, two levels of quoting are added around each element.

An actual implementation of these three macros is distributed as m4-1.4.17/examples/ quote.m4 in this package. First, let's examine their usage:

```
$ m4 -I examples
include('quote.m4')
⇒
-quote-dquote-dquote_elt-
⇒----
-quote()-dquote()-dquote_elt()-
⇒--''-''-
-quote('1')-dquote('1')-dquote_elt('1')-
⇒-1-'1'-'1'-
-quote('1', '2')-dquote('1', '2')-dquote_elt('1', '2')-
⇒-1,2-'1','2'-'1','2'-
define('n', '$#')dnl
```

```
-n(quote('1', '2'))-n(dquote('1', '2'))-n(dquote_elt('1', '2'))-
⇒-1-1-2-
dquote(dquote_elt('1', '2'))
⇒''1'',''2''
dquote_elt(dquote('1', '2'))
⇒''1','2''
```

The last two lines show that when given two arguments, dquote results in one string, while dquote_elt results in two. Now, examine the implementation. Note that quote and dquote_elt make decisions based on their number of arguments, so that when called without arguments, they result in nothing instead of a quoted empty string; this is so that it is possible to distinguish between no arguments and an empty first argument. dquote, on the other hand, results in a string no matter what, since it is still possible to tell whether it was invoked without arguments based on the resulting string.

```
$ m4 -I examples
undivert('quote.m4')dnl
⇒divert('-1')
⇒# quote(args) - convert args to single-quoted string
⇒define('quote', 'ifelse('$#', '0', '', ''$*'')')
⇒# dquote(args) - convert args to quoted list of quoted strings
⇒define('dquote', ''$@'')
⇒# dquote_elt(args) - convert args to list of double-quoted strings
⇒define('dquote_elt', 'ifelse('$#', '0', '', '$#', '1', '''$1''',
⇒                            '''$1'',$0(shift($@))')')
⇒divert''dnl
```

It is worth pointing out that 'quote(*args*)' is more efficient than 'joinall(',', *args*)' for producing the same output.

One more useful macro based on shift allows portably selecting an arbitrary argument (usually greater than the ninth argument), without relying on the GNU extension of multi-digit arguments (see Section 5.2 [Arguments], page 26).

argn (*n*, ...)   [Composite]

> Expands to argument *n* out of the remaining arguments. *n* must be a positive number. Usually invoked as 'argn('*n*',$@)'.

It is implemented as:

```
define('argn', 'ifelse('$1', 1, ''$2'',
  'argn(decr('$1'), shift(shift($@)))')')
⇒
argn('1', 'a')
⇒a
define('foo', 'argn('11', $@)')
⇒
foo('a', 'b', 'c', 'd', 'e', 'f', 'g', 'h', 'i', 'j', 'k', 'l')
⇒k
```

6.4 Iteration by counting

Here is an example of a loop macro that implements a simple for loop.

forloop (*iterator*, *start*, *end*, *text*)   [Composite]

    Takes the name in *iterator*, which must be a valid macro name, and successively assign it each integer value from *start* to *end*, inclusive. For each assignment to *iterator*, append *text* to the expansion of the **forloop**. *text* may refer to *iterator*. Any definition of *iterator* prior to this invocation is restored.

It can, for example, be used for simple counting:

```
$ m4 -I examples
include('forloop.m4')
⇒
forloop('i', '1', '8', 'i ')
⇒1 2 3 4 5 6 7 8
```

For-loops can be nested, like:

```
$ m4 -I examples
include('forloop.m4')
⇒
forloop('i', '1', '4', 'forloop('j', '1', '8', ' (i, j)')
')
⇒ (1, 1) (1, 2) (1, 3) (1, 4) (1, 5) (1, 6) (1, 7) (1, 8)
⇒ (2, 1) (2, 2) (2, 3) (2, 4) (2, 5) (2, 6) (2, 7) (2, 8)
⇒ (3, 1) (3, 2) (3, 3) (3, 4) (3, 5) (3, 6) (3, 7) (3, 8)
⇒ (4, 1) (4, 2) (4, 3) (4, 4) (4, 5) (4, 6) (4, 7) (4, 8)
⇒
```

The implementation of the **forloop** macro is fairly straightforward. The **forloop** macro itself is simply a wrapper, which saves the previous definition of the first argument, calls the internal macro **_forloop**, and re-establishes the saved definition of the first argument.

The macro **_forloop** expands the fourth argument once, and tests to see if the iterator has reached the final value. If it has not finished, it increments the iterator (using the predefined macro **incr**, see Section 12.1 [Incr], page 89), and recurses.

Here is an actual implementation of **forloop**, distributed as **m4-1.4.17/examples/forloop.m4** in this package:

```
$ m4 -I examples
undivert('forloop.m4')dnl
⇒divert('-1')
⇒# forloop(var, from, to, stmt) - simple version
⇒define('forloop', 'pushdef('$1', '$2')_forloop($@)popdef('$1')')
⇒define('_forloop',
⇒        '$4''ifelse($1, '$3', '', 'define('$1', incr($1))$0($@)')')
⇒divert''dnl
```

Notice the careful use of quotes. Certain macro arguments are left unquoted, each for its own reason. Try to find out *why* these arguments are left unquoted, and see what happens if they are quoted. (As presented, these two macros are useful but not very robust for general use. They lack even basic error handling for cases like *start* less than *end*, *end* not numeric, or *iterator* not being a macro name. See if you can improve these macros; or see Section 17.2 [Answers], page 115).

6.5 Iteration by list contents

Here is an example of a loop macro that implements list iteration.

foreach (*iterator*, *paren-list*, *text*)   [Composite]
foreachq (*iterator*, *quote-list*, *text*)   [Composite]
>   Takes the name in *iterator*, which must be a valid macro name, and successively assign it each value from *paren-list* or *quote-list*. In foreach, *paren-list* is a comma-separated list of elements contained in parentheses. In foreachq, *quote-list* is a comma-separated list of elements contained in a quoted string. For each assignment to *iterator*, append *text* to the overall expansion. *text* may refer to *iterator*. Any definition of *iterator* prior to this invocation is restored.

As an example, this displays each word in a list inside of a sentence, using an implementation of foreach distributed as m4-1.4.17/examples/foreach.m4, and foreachq in m4-1.4.17/examples/foreachq.m4.

```
$ m4 -I examples
include('foreach.m4')
⇒
foreach('x', (foo, bar, foobar), 'Word was: x
')dnl
⇒Word was: foo
⇒Word was: bar
⇒Word was: foobar
include('foreachq.m4')
⇒
foreachq('x', 'foo, bar, foobar', 'Word was: x
')dnl
⇒Word was: foo
⇒Word was: bar
⇒Word was: foobar
```

It is possible to be more complex; each element of the *paren-list* or *quote-list* can itself be a list, to pass as further arguments to a helper macro. This example generates a shell case statement:

```
$ m4 -I examples
include('foreach.m4')
⇒
define('_case', '  $1)
    $2=" $1";;
')dnl
define('_cat', '$1$2')dnl
case $''1 in
⇒case $1 in
```

```
foreach('x', '('('a', 'vara')', '('b', 'varb')', '('c', 'varc')')',
        '_cat('_case', x)')dnl
⇒  a)
⇒    vara=" a";;
⇒  b)
⇒    varb=" b";;
⇒  c)
⇒    varc=" c";;
esac
⇒esac
```

The implementation of the `foreach` macro is a bit more involved; it is a wrapper around two helper macros. First, `_arg1` is needed to grab the first element of a list. Second, `_foreach` implements the recursion, successively walking through the original list. Here is a simple implementation of `foreach`:

```
$ m4 -I examples
undivert('foreach.m4')dnl
⇒divert('-1')
⇒# foreach(x, (item_1, item_2, ..., item_n), stmt)
⇒#   parenthesized list, simple version
⇒define('foreach', 'pushdef('$1')_foreach($@)popdef('$1')')
⇒define('_arg1', '$1')
⇒define('_foreach', 'ifelse('$2', '()', '',
⇒  'define('$1', _arg1$2)$3''$0('$1', (shift$2), '$3')')')
⇒divert''dnl
```

Unfortunately, that implementation is not robust to macro names as list elements. Each iteration of `_foreach` is stripping another layer of quotes, leading to erratic results if list elements are not already fully expanded. The first cut at implementing `foreachq` takes this into account. Also, when using quoted elements in a *paren-list*, the overall list must be quoted. A *quote-list* has the nice property of requiring fewer characters to create a list containing the same quoted elements. To see the difference between the two macros, we attempt to pass double-quoted macro names in a list, expecting the macro name on output after one layer of quotes is removed during list iteration and the final layer removed during the final rescan:

```
$ m4 -I examples
define('a', '1')define('b', '2')define('c', '3')
⇒
include('foreach.m4')
⇒
include('foreachq.m4')
⇒
foreach('x', '(''a'', ''(b'', ''c)'')', 'x
')
⇒1
⇒(2)1
⇒
⇒, x
```

```
⇒)
foreachq('x', '''a'', ''(b'', ''c)''', 'x
')dnl
⇒a
⇒(b
⇒c)
```

Obviously, `foreachq` did a better job; here is its implementation:

```
$ m4 -I examples
undivert('foreachq.m4')dnl
⇒include('quote.m4')dnl
⇒divert('-1')
⇒# foreachq(x, 'item_1, item_2, ..., item_n', stmt)
⇒#   quoted list, simple version
⇒define('foreachq', 'pushdef('$1')_foreachq($@)popdef('$1')')
⇒define('_arg1', '$1')
⇒define('_foreachq', 'ifelse(quote($2), '', '',
⇒  'define('$1', '_arg1($2)')$3''$0('$1', 'shift($2)', '$3')')')
⇒divert''dnl
```

Notice that `_foreachq` had to use the helper macro `quote` defined earlier (see Section 6.3 [Shift], page 41), to ensure that the embedded `ifelse` call does not go haywire if a list element contains a comma. Unfortunately, this implementation of `foreachq` has its own severe flaw. Whereas the `foreach` implementation was linear, this macro is quadratic in the number of list elements, and is much more likely to trip up the limit set by the command line option `--nesting-limit` (or `-L`, see Section 2.3 [Invoking m4], page 10). Additionally, this implementation does not expand '`defn('iterator')`' very well, when compared with `foreach`.

```
$ m4 -I examples
include('foreach.m4')include('foreachq.m4')
⇒
foreach('name', '('a', 'b')', ' defn('name')')
⇒ a b
foreachq('name', ''a', 'b'', ' defn('name')')
⇒ _arg1('a', 'b') _arg1(shift('a', 'b'))
```

It is possible to have robust iteration with linear behavior and sane *iterator* contents for either list style. See if you can learn from the best elements of both of these implementations to create robust macros (or see Section 17.3 [Answers], page 117).

6.6 Working with definition stacks

Thanks to `pushdef`, manipulation of a stack is an intrinsic operation in `m4`. Normally, only the topmost definition in a stack is important, but sometimes, it is desirable to manipulate the entire definition stack.

stack_foreach (*macro*, *action*)   [Composite]
stack_foreach_lifo (*macro*, *action*)   [Composite]
>   For each of the `pushdef` definitions associated with *macro*, invoke the macro *action* with a single argument of that definition. `stack_foreach` visits the oldest definition

first, while `stack_foreach_lifo` visits the current definition first. *action* should not modify or dereference *macro*. There are a few special macros, such as `defn`, which cannot be used as the *macro* parameter.

A sample implementation of these macros is distributed in the file `m4-1.4.17/examples/stack.m4`.

```
$ m4 -I examples
include('stack.m4')
⇒
pushdef('a', '1')pushdef('a', '2')pushdef('a', '3')
⇒
define('show', '`$1'
')
⇒
stack_foreach('a', 'show')dnl
⇒1
⇒2
⇒3
stack_foreach_lifo('a', 'show')dnl
⇒3
⇒2
⇒1
```

Now for the implementation. Note the definition of a helper macro, `_stack_reverse`, which destructively swaps the contents of one stack of definitions into the reverse order in the temporary macro 'tmp-$1'. By calling the helper twice, the original order is restored back into the macro '$1'; since the operation is destructive, this explains why '$1' must not be modified or dereferenced during the traversal. The caller can then inject additional code to pass the definition currently being visited to '$2'. The choice of helper names is intentional; since '-' is not valid as part of a macro name, there is no risk of conflict with a valid macro name, and the code is guaranteed to use `defn` where necessary. Finally, note that any macro used in the traversal of a `pushdef` stack, such as `pushdef` or `defn`, cannot be handled by `stack_foreach`, since the macro would temporarily be undefined during the algorithm.

```
$ m4 -I examples
undivert('stack.m4')dnl
⇒divert('-1')
⇒# stack_foreach(macro, action)
⇒# Invoke ACTION with a single argument of each definition
⇒# from the definition stack of MACRO, starting with the oldest.
⇒define('stack_foreach',
⇒'_stack_reverse('$1', 'tmp-$1')'dnl
⇒'_stack_reverse('tmp-$1', '$1', '$2(defn('$1'))')')
⇒# stack_foreach_lifo(macro, action)
⇒# Invoke ACTION with a single argument of each definition
⇒# from the definition stack of MACRO, starting with the newest.
⇒define('stack_foreach_lifo',
⇒'_stack_reverse('$1', 'tmp-$1', '$2(defn('$1'))')'dnl
```

```
⇒'_stack_reverse('tmp-$1', '$1')')
⇒define('_stack_reverse',
⇒'ifdef('$1', 'pushdef('$2', defn('$1'))$3''popdef('$1')$0($@)')')
⇒divert''dnl
```

6.7 Building macros with macros

Since m4 is a macro language, it is possible to write macros that can build other macros. First on the list is a way to automate the creation of blind macros.

define_blind (*name*, [*value*])   [Composite]

    Defines *name* as a blind macro, such that *name* will expand to *value* only when given explicit arguments. *value* should not be the result of **defn** (see Section 5.5 [Defn], page 31). This macro is only recognized with parameters, and results in an empty string.

Defining a macro to define another macro can be a bit tricky. We want to use a literal '$#' in the argument to the nested **define**. However, if '$' and '#' are adjacent in the definition of **define_blind**, then it would be expanded as the number of arguments to **define_blind** rather than the intended number of arguments to *name*. The solution is to pass the difficult characters through extra arguments to a helper macro **_define_blind**. When composing macros, it is a common idiom to need a helper macro to concatenate text that forms parameters in the composed macro, rather than interpreting the text as a parameter of the composing macro.

As for the limitation against using **defn**, there are two reasons. If a macro was previously defined with **define_blind**, then it can safely be renamed to a new blind macro using plain **define**; using **define_blind** to rename it just adds another layer of **ifelse**, occupying memory and slowing down execution. And if a macro is a builtin, then it would result in an attempt to define a macro consisting of both text and a builtin token; this is not supported, and the builtin token is flattened to an empty string.

With that explanation, here's the definition, and some sample usage. Notice that **define_blind** is itself a blind macro.

```
$ m4 -d
define('define_blind', 'ifelse('$#', '0', ''$0'',
'_$0('$1', '$2', '$''#', '$''0')')')
⇒
define('_define_blind', 'define('$1',
'ifelse('$3', '0', ''$4'', '$2')')')
⇒
define_blind
⇒define_blind
define_blind('foo', 'arguments were $*')
⇒
foo
⇒foo
foo('bar')
⇒arguments were bar
```

```
define('blah', defn('foo'))
⇒
blah
⇒blah
blah('a', 'b')
⇒arguments were a,b
defn('blah')
⇒ifelse('$#', '0', ''$0'', 'arguments were $*')
```

Another interesting composition tactic is argument *currying*, or factoring a macro that takes multiple arguments for use in a context that provides exactly one argument.

curry (*macro*, ...)   [Composite]

    Expand to a macro call that takes exactly one argument, then appends that argument to the original arguments and invokes *macro* with the resulting list of arguments.

A demonstration of currying makes the intent of this macro a little more obvious. The macro **stack_foreach** mentioned earlier is an example of a context that provides exactly one argument to a macro name. But coupled with currying, we can invoke **reverse** with two arguments for each definition of a macro stack. This example uses the file m4-1.4.17/ examples/curry.m4 included in the distribution.

```
$ m4 -I examples
include('curry.m4')include('stack.m4')
⇒
define('reverse', 'ifelse('$#', '0', , '$#', '1', ''$1'',
                          'reverse(shift($@)), '$1'')')
⇒
pushdef('a', '1')pushdef('a', '2')pushdef('a', '3')
⇒
stack_foreach('a', ':curry('reverse', '4')')
⇒:1, 4:2, 4:3, 4
curry('curry', 'reverse', '1')('2')('3')
⇒3, 2, 1
```

Now for the implementation. Notice how **curry** leaves off with a macro name but no open parenthesis, while still in the middle of collecting arguments for '$1'. The macro **_curry** is the helper macro that takes one argument, then adds it to the list and finally supplies the closing parenthesis. The use of a comma inside the **shift** call allows currying to also work for a macro that takes one argument, although it often makes more sense to invoke that macro directly rather than going through **curry**.

```
$ m4 -I examples
undivert('curry.m4')dnl
⇒divert('-1')
⇒# curry(macro, args)
⇒# Expand to a macro call that takes one argument, then invoke
⇒# macro(args, extra).
⇒define('curry', '$1(shift($@,)_$0')
⇒define('_curry', ''$1')')
⇒divert''dnl
```

Unfortunately, with M4 1.4.x, `curry` is unable to handle builtin tokens, which are silently flattened to the empty string when passed through another text macro. This limitation will be lifted in a future release of M4.

Putting the last few concepts together, it is possible to copy or rename an entire stack of macro definitions.

copy (*source*, *dest*)   [Composite]
rename (*source*, *dest*)   [Composite]

> Ensure that *dest* is undefined, then define it to the same stack of definitions currently in *source*. `copy` leaves *source* unchanged, while `rename` undefines *source*. There are only a few macros, such as `copy` or `defn`, which cannot be copied via this macro.

The implementation is relatively straightforward (although since it uses `curry`, it is unable to copy builtin macros, such as the second definition of a as a synonym for `divnum`. See if you can design a version that works around this limitation, or see Section 17.4 [Answers], page 124).

```
$ m4 -I examples
include('curry.m4')include('stack.m4')
⇒
define('rename', 'copy($@)undefine('$1')')dnl
define('copy', 'ifdef('$2', 'errprint('$2 already defined
')m4exit('1')',
    'stack_foreach('$1', 'curry('pushdef', '$2')')')')dnl
pushdef('a', '1')pushdef('a', defn('divnum'))pushdef('a', '2')
⇒
copy('a', 'b')
⇒
rename('b', 'c')
⇒
a b c
⇒2 b 2
popdef('a', 'c')c a
⇒ 0
popdef('a', 'c')a c
⇒1 1
```

7 How to debug macros and input

When writing macros for m4, they often do not work as intended on the first try (as is the case with most programming languages). Fortunately, there is support for macro debugging in m4.

7.1 Displaying macro definitions

If you want to see what a name expands into, you can use the builtin dumpdef:

dumpdef ([*names...*])   [Builtin]

Accepts any number of arguments. If called without any arguments, it displays the definitions of all known names, otherwise it displays the definitions of the *names* given. The output is printed to the current debug file (usually standard error), and is sorted by name. If an unknown name is encountered, a warning is printed.

The expansion of dumpdef is void.

```
$ m4 -d
define('foo', 'Hello world.')
⇒
dumpdef('foo')
error  foo: 'Hello world.'
⇒
dumpdef('define')
error  define: <define>
⇒
```

The last example shows how builtin macros definitions are displayed. The definition that is dumped corresponds to what would occur if the macro were to be called at that point, even if other definitions are still live due to redefining a macro during argument collection.

```
$ m4 -d
pushdef('f', ''$0'1')pushdef('f', ''$0'2')
⇒
f(popdef('f')dumpdef('f'))
error  f: ''$0'1'
⇒f2
f(popdef('f')dumpdef('f'))
error  m4:stdin:3: undefined macro 'f'
⇒f1
```

See Section 7.3 [Debug Levels], page 58, for information on controlling the details of the display.

7.2 Tracing macro calls

It is possible to trace macro calls and expansions through the builtins traceon and traceoff:

traceon ([*names...*])   [Builtin]
traceoff ([*names...*])   [Builtin]
> When called without any arguments, `traceon` and `traceoff` will turn tracing on and
> off, respectively, for all currently defined macros.
>
> When called with arguments, only the macros listed in *names* are affected, whether
> or not they are currently defined.
>
> The expansion of `traceon` and `traceoff` is void.

Whenever a traced macro is called and the arguments have been collected, the call is
displayed. If the expansion of the macro call is not void, the expansion can be displayed
after the call. The output is printed to the current debug file (defaulting to standard error,
see Section 7.4 [Debug Output], page 60).

```
$ m4 -d
define('foo', 'Hello World.')
⇒
define('echo', '$@')
⇒
traceon('foo', 'echo')
⇒
foo
error m4trace: -1- foo -> 'Hello World.'
⇒Hello World.
echo('gnus', 'and gnats')
error m4trace: -1- echo('gnus', 'and gnats') -> ''gnus','and gnats''
⇒gnus,and gnats
```

The number between dashes is the depth of the expansion. It is one most of the time,
signifying an expansion at the outermost level, but it increases when macro arguments
contain unquoted macro calls. The maximum number that will appear between dashes is
controlled by the option `--nesting-limit` (or `-L`, see Section 2.3 [Invoking m4], page 10).
Additionally, the option `--trace` (or `-t`) can be used to invoke `traceon(name)` before
parsing input.

```
$ m4 -L 3 -t ifelse
ifelse('one level')
error m4trace: -1- ifelse
⇒
ifelse(ifelse(ifelse('three levels')))
error m4trace: -3- ifelse
error m4trace: -2- ifelse
error m4trace: -1- ifelse
⇒
ifelse(ifelse(ifelse(ifelse('four levels'))))
error m4:stdin:3: recursion limit of 3 exceeded, use -L<N> to change it
```

Tracing by name is an attribute that is preserved whether the macro is defined or not.
This allows the selection of macros to trace before those macros are defined.

```
$ m4 -d
traceoff('foo')
```

```
⇒
traceon('foo')
⇒
foo
⇒foo
defn('foo')
⇒
define('foo', 'bar')
⇒
foo
[error] m4trace: -1- foo -> 'bar'
⇒bar
undefine('foo')
⇒
ifdef('foo', 'yes', 'no')
⇒no
indir('foo')
[error] m4:stdin:9: undefined macro 'foo'
⇒
define('foo', 'blah')
⇒
foo
[error] m4trace: -1- foo -> 'blah'
⇒blah
traceoff
⇒
foo
⇒blah
```

Tracing even works on builtins. However, **defn** (see Section 5.5 [Defn], page 31) does not transfer tracing status.

```
$ m4 -d
traceon('traceon')
⇒
traceon('traceoff')
[error] m4trace: -1- traceon('traceoff')
⇒
traceoff('traceoff')
[error] m4trace: -1- traceoff('traceoff')
⇒
traceoff('traceon')
⇒
traceon('eval', 'm4_divnum')
⇒
define('m4_eval', defn('eval'))
⇒
define('m4_divnum', defn('divnum'))
```

```
⇒
eval(divnum)
error m4trace: -1- eval('0') -> '0'
⇒0
m4_eval(m4_divnum)
error m4trace: -2- m4_divnum -> '0'
⇒0
```

See Section 7.3 [Debug Levels], page 58, for information on controlling the details of the display. The format of the trace output is not specified by POSIX, and varies between implementations of m4.

7.3 Controlling debugging output

The -d option to m4 (or --debug, see Section 2.5 [Invoking m4], page 11) controls the amount of details presented in three categories of output. Trace output is requested by traceon (see Section 7.2 [Trace], page 55), and each line is prefixed by 'm4trace:' in relation to a macro invocation. Debug output tracks useful events not associated with a macro invocation, and each line is prefixed by 'm4debug:'. Finally, dumpdef (see Section 7.1 [Dumpdef], page 55) output is affected, with no prefix added to the output lines.

The *flags* following the option can be one or more of the following:

a   In trace output, show the actual arguments that were collected before invoking the macro. This applies to all macro calls if the 't' flag is used, otherwise only the macros covered by calls of traceon. Arguments are subject to length truncation specified by the command line option --arglength (or -l).

c   In trace output, show several trace lines for each macro call. A line is shown when the macro is seen, but before the arguments are collected; a second line when the arguments have been collected and a third line after the call has completed.

e   In trace output, show the expansion of each macro call, if it is not void. This applies to all macro calls if the 't' flag is used, otherwise only the macros covered by calls of traceon. The expansion is subject to length truncation specified by the command line option --arglength (or -l).

f   In debug and trace output, include the name of the current input file in the output line.

i   In debug output, print a message each time the current input file is changed.

l   In debug and trace output, include the current input line number in the output line.

p   In debug output, print a message when a named file is found through the path search mechanism (see Section 9.2 [Search Path], page 74), giving the actual file name used.

q   In trace and dumpdef output, quote actual arguments and macro expansions in the display with the current quotes. This is useful in connection with the 'a' and 'e' flags above.

t   In trace output, trace all macro calls made in this invocation of m4, regardless
            of the settings of traceon.

x   In trace output, add a unique 'macro call id' to each line of the trace output.
            This is useful in connection with the 'c' flag above.

V   A shorthand for all of the above flags.

If no flags are specified with the -d option, the default is 'aeq'. The examples throughout
this manual assume the default flags.

There is a builtin macro debugmode, which allows on-the-fly control of the debugging
output format:

debugmode ([*flags*])   [Builtin]
    The argument *flags* should be a subset of the letters listed above. As special cases, if
    the argument starts with a '+', the flags are added to the current debug flags, and if
    it starts with a '-', they are removed. If no argument is present, all debugging flags
    are cleared (as if no -d was given), and with an empty argument the flags are reset
    to the default of 'aeq'.

    The expansion of debugmode is void.

    ```
    $ m4
    define('foo', 'FOO')
    ⇒
    traceon('foo')
    ⇒
    debugmode()
    ⇒
    foo
    error m4trace: -1- foo -> 'FOO'
    ⇒FOO
    debugmode
    ⇒
    foo
    error m4trace: -1- foo
    ⇒FOO
    debugmode('+l')
    ⇒
    foo
    error m4trace:8: -1- foo
    ⇒FOO
    ```

The following example demonstrates the behavior of length truncation, when specified on
the command line. Note that each argument and the final result are individually truncated.
Also, the special tokens for builtin functions are not truncated.

```
$ m4 -d -l 6
define('echo', '$@')debugmode('+t')
⇒
echo('1', 'long string')
error m4trace: -1- echo('1', 'long s...') -> ''1','l...'
```

```
⇒1,long string
indir('echo', defn('changequote'))
error  m4trace: -2- defn('change...')
error  m4trace: -1- indir('echo', <changequote>) -> '' ''
⇒
```

This example shows the effects of the debug flags that are not related to macro tracing.

```
$ m4 -dip -I examples
error  m4debug: input read from stdin
include('foo')dnl
error  m4debug: path search for 'foo' found 'examples/foo'
error  m4debug: input read from examples/foo
⇒bar
error  m4debug: input reverted to stdin, line 1
^D
error  m4debug: input exhausted
```

7.4 Saving debugging output

Debug and tracing output can be redirected to files using either the `--debugfile` option to `m4` (see Section 2.5 [Invoking m4], page 11), or with the builtin macro `debugfile`:

debugfile ([*file*])   [Builtin]

Sends all further debug and trace output to *file*, opened in append mode. If *file* is the empty string, debug and trace output are discarded. If `debugfile` is called without any arguments, debug and trace output are sent to standard error. This does not affect warnings, error messages, or `errprint` output, which are always sent to standard error. If *file* cannot be opened, the current debug file is unchanged, and an error is issued.

The expansion of `debugfile` is void.

```
$ m4 -d
traceon('divnum')
⇒
divnum('extra')
error  m4:stdin:2: Warning: excess arguments to builtin 'divnum' ignored
error  m4trace: -1- divnum('extra') -> '0'
⇒0
debugfile()
⇒
divnum('extra')
error  m4:stdin:4: Warning: excess arguments to builtin 'divnum' ignored
⇒0
debugfile
⇒
divnum
error  m4trace: -1- divnum -> '0'
⇒0
```

8 Input control

This chapter describes various builtin macros for controlling the input to m4.

8.1 Deleting whitespace in input

The builtin dnl stands for "Discard to Next Line":

dnl   [Builtin]
> All characters, up to and including the next newline, are discarded without performing any macro expansion. A warning is issued if the end of the file is encountered without a newline.
>
> The expansion of dnl is void.

It is often used in connection with define, to remove the newline that follows the call to define. Thus

```
define('foo', 'Macro 'foo'.')dnl A very simple macro, indeed.
foo
⇒Macro foo.
```

The input up to and including the next newline is discarded, as opposed to the way comments are treated (see Section 3.3 [Comments], page 15).

Usually, dnl is immediately followed by an end of line or some other whitespace. GNU m4 will produce a warning diagnostic if dnl is followed by an open parenthesis. In this case, dnl will collect and process all arguments, looking for a matching close parenthesis. All predictable side effects resulting from this collection will take place. dnl will return no output. The input following the matching close parenthesis up to and including the next newline, on whatever line containing it, will still be discarded.

```
dnl('args are ignored, but side effects occur',
define('foo', 'like this')) while this text is ignored: undefine('foo')
error m4:stdin:1: Warning: excess arguments to builtin 'dnl' ignored
See how 'foo' was defined, foo?
⇒See how foo was defined, like this?
```

If the end of file is encountered without a newline character, a warning is issued and dnl stops consuming input.

```
m4wrap('m4wrap('2 hi
')0 hi dnl 1 hi')
⇒
define('hi', 'HI')
⇒
^D
error m4:stdin:1: Warning: end of file treated as newline
⇒0 HI 2 HI
```

8.2 Changing the quote characters

The default quote delimiters can be changed with the builtin `changequote`:

changequote ([*start* = "'], [*end* = ''])   [Builtin]

> This sets *start* as the new begin-quote delimiter and *end* as the new end-quote de-
> limiter. If both arguments are missing, the default quotes (' and ') are used. If *start*
> is void, then quoting is disabled. Otherwise, if *end* is missing or void, the default
> end-quote delimiter (') is used. The quote delimiters can be of any length.
>
> The expansion of `changequote` is void.
>
> ```
> changequote('[', ']')
> ⇒
> define([foo], [Macro [foo].])
> ⇒
> foo
> ⇒Macro foo.
> ```

The quotation strings can safely contain eight-bit characters. If no single character is
appropriate, *start* and *end* can be of any length. Other implementations cap the delimiter
length to five characters, but GNU has no inherent limit.

```
changequote('[[[', ']]]')
⇒
define([[[foo]]], [[[Macro [[[[[foo]]]]].]]])
⇒
foo
⇒Macro [[foo]].
```

Calling `changequote` with *start* as the empty string will effectively disable the quoting
mechanism, leaving no way to quote text. However, using an empty string is not portable,
as some other implementations of `m4` revert to the default quoting, while others preserve the
prior non-empty delimiter. If *start* is not empty, then an empty *end* will use the default end-
quote delimiter of '', as otherwise, it would be impossible to end a quoted string. Again,
this is not portable, as some other `m4` implementations reuse *start* as the end-quote delimiter,
while others preserve the previous non-empty value. Omitting both arguments restores the
default begin-quote and end-quote delimiters; fortunately this behavior is portable to all
implementations of `m4`.

```
define('foo', 'Macro 'FOO'.')
⇒
changequote('', '')
⇒
foo
⇒Macro 'FOO'.
'foo'
⇒'Macro 'FOO'.'
changequote(',)
⇒
foo
⇒Macro FOO.
```

There is no way in `m4` to quote a string containing an unmatched begin-quote, except using `changequote` to change the current quotes.

If the quotes should be changed from, say, '[' to '[[', temporary quote characters have to be defined. To achieve this, two calls of `changequote` must be made, one for the temporary quotes and one for the new quotes.

Macros are recognized in preference to the begin-quote string, so if a prefix of *start* can be recognized as part of a potential macro name, the quoting mechanism is effectively disabled. Unless you use `changeword` (see Section 8.4 [Changeword], page 67), this means that *start* should not begin with a letter, digit, or '_' (underscore). However, even though quoted strings are not recognized, the quote characters can still be discerned in macro expansion and in trace output.

```
define('echo', '$@')
⇒
define('hi', 'HI')
⇒
changequote('q', 'Q')
⇒
q hi Q hi
⇒q HI Q HI
echo(hi)
⇒qHIQ
changequote
⇒
changequote('-', 'EOF')
⇒
- hi EOF hi
⇒ hi   HI
changequote
⇒
changequote('1', '2')
⇒
hi1hi2
⇒hi1hi2
hi 1hi2
⇒HI hi
```

Quotes are recognized in preference to argument collection. In particular, if *start* is a single '(', then argument collection is effectively disabled. For portability with other implementations, it is a good idea to avoid '(', ',', and ')' as the first character in *start*.

```
define('echo', '$#:$@:')
⇒
define('hi', 'HI')
⇒
changequote('(',')')
⇒
echo(hi)
⇒0::hi
```

```
changequote
⇒
changequote('((', '))')
⇒
echo(hi)
⇒1:HI:
echo((hi))
⇒0::hi
changequote
⇒
changequote(',', ')')
⇒
echo(hi,hi)bye)
⇒1:HIhibye:
```

However, if you are not worried about portability, using '(' and ')' as quoting characters
has an interesting property—you can use it to compute a quoted string containing the
expansion of any quoted text, as long as the expansion results in both balanced quotes
and balanced parentheses. The trick is realizing **expand** uses '$1' unquoted, to trigger
its expansion using the normal quoting characters, but uses extra parentheses to group
unquoted commas that occur in the expansion without consuming whitespace following
those commas. Then **_expand** uses **changequote** to convert the extra parentheses back
into quoting characters. Note that it takes two more **changequote** invocations to restore
the original quotes. Contrast the behavior on whitespace when using '$*', via **quote**, to
attempt the same task.

```
changequote('[', ']')dnl
define([a], [1, (b)])dnl
define([b], [2])dnl
define([quote], [[$*]])dnl
define([expand], [_$0(($1))])dnl
define([_expand],
  [changequote([(], [)])$1changequote''changequote('[', ']')])dnl
expand([a, a, [a, a], [[a, a]]])
⇒1, (2), 1, (2), a, a, [a, a]
quote(a, a, [a, a], [[a, a]])
⇒1,(2),1,(2),a, a,[a, a]
```

If *end* is a prefix of *start*, the end-quote will be recognized in preference to a nested
begin-quote. In particular, changing the quotes to have the same string for *start* and *end*
disables nesting of quotes. When quote nesting is disabled, it is impossible to double-quote
strings across macro expansions, so using the same string is not done very often.

```
define('hi', 'HI')
⇒
changequote('"', '"')
⇒
""hi"""hi"
⇒hihi
""hi" ""hi"
```

```
⇒hi hi
""hi"" "hi"
⇒hi" "HI"
changequote
⇒
'hi'hi'hi'
⇒hi'hi'hi
changequote('"', '"')
⇒
"hi"hi"hi"
⇒hiHIhi
```

It is an error if the end of file occurs within a quoted string.

```
'hello world'
⇒hello world
'dangling quote
^D
error m4:stdin:2: ERROR: end of file in string
ifelse('dangling quote
^D
error m4:stdin:1: ERROR: end of file in string
```

8.3 Changing the comment delimiters

The default comment delimiters can be changed with the builtin macro **changecom**:

changecom ([start], [end = 'NL'])   [Builtin]

> This sets *start* as the new begin-comment delimiter and *end* as the new end-comment delimiter. If both arguments are missing, or *start* is void, then comments are disabled. Otherwise, if *end* is missing or void, the default end-comment delimiter of newline is used. The comment delimiters can be of any length.
>
> The expansion of **changecom** is void.
>
> ```
> define('comment', 'COMMENT')
> ⇒
> # A normal comment
> ⇒# A normal comment
> changecom('/*', '*/')
> ⇒
> # Not a comment anymore
> ⇒# Not a COMMENT anymore
> But: /* this is a comment now */ while this is not a comment
> ⇒But: /* this is a comment now */ while this is not a COMMENT
> ```

Note how comments are copied to the output, much as if they were quoted strings. If you want the text inside a comment expanded, quote the begin-comment delimiter.

Calling **changecom** without any arguments, or with *start* as the empty string, will effectively disable the commenting mechanism. To restore the original comment start of '#', you must explicitly ask for it. If *start* is not empty, then an empty *end* will use the default end-comment delimiter of newline, as otherwise, it would be impossible to end a comment. However, this is not portable, as some other `m4` implementations preserve the previous non-empty delimiters instead.

```
define('comment', 'COMMENT')
⇒
changecom
⇒
# Not a comment anymore
⇒# Not a COMMENT anymore
changecom('#', '')
⇒
# comment again
⇒# comment again
```

The comment strings can safely contain eight-bit characters. If no single character is appropriate, *start* and *end* can be of any length. Other implementations cap the delimiter length to five characters, but GNU has no inherent limit.

Comments are recognized in preference to macros. However, this is not compatible with other implementations, where macros and even quoting takes precedence over comments, so it may change in a future release. For portability, this means that *start* should not begin with a letter, digit, or '_' (underscore), and that neither the start-quote nor the start-comment string should be a prefix of the other.

```
define('hi', 'HI')
⇒
define('hi1hi2', 'hello')
⇒
changecom('q', 'Q')
⇒
q hi Q hi
⇒q hi Q HI
changecom('1', '2')
⇒
hi1hi2
⇒hello
hi 1hi2
⇒HI 1hi2
```

Comments are recognized in preference to argument collection. In particular, if *start* is a single '(', then argument collection is effectively disabled. For portability with other implementations, it is a good idea to avoid '(', ',', and ')' as the first character in *start*.

```
define('echo', '$#:$*:$@:')
⇒
define('hi', 'HI')
⇒
changecom('(',')')
⇒
echo(hi)
```

```
⇒0:::(hi)
changecom
⇒
changecom('((', '))')
⇒
echo(hi)
⇒1:HI:HI:
echo((hi))
⇒0:::((hi))
changecom(',', ')')
⇒
echo(hi,hi)bye)
⇒1:HI,hi)bye:HI,hi)bye:
changecom
⇒
echo(hi,',''hi',hi)
⇒3:HI,,HI,HI:HI,,''hi,HI:
echo(hi,',''hi',hi''changecom(',,', 'hi'))
⇒3:HI,,''hi,HI:HI,,''hi,HI:
```

It is an error if the end of file occurs within a comment.

```
changecom('/*', '*/')
⇒
/*dangling comment
^D
error m4:stdin:2: ERROR: end of file in comment
```

8.4 Changing the lexical structure of words

The macro `changeword` and all associated functionality is experimental. It is only available if the `--enable-changeword` option was given to `configure`, at GNU `m4` installation time. The functionality will go away in the future, to be replaced by other new features that are more efficient at providing the same capabilities. *Do not rely on it.* Please direct your comments about it the same way you would do for bugs.

A file being processed by `m4` is split into quoted strings, words (potential macro names) and simple tokens (any other single character). Initially a word is defined by the following regular expression:

```
[_a-zA-Z][_a-zA-Z0-9]*
```

Using `changeword`, you can change this regular expression:

changeword (*regex*)   [Optional builtin]

Changes the regular expression for recognizing macro names to be *regex*. If *regex* is empty, use '`[_a-zA-Z][_a-zA-Z0-9]*`'. *regex* must obey the constraint that every prefix of the desired final pattern is also accepted by the regular expression. If *regex* contains grouping parentheses, the macro invoked is the portion that matched the first group, rather than the entire matching string.

The expansion of `changeword` is void. The macro `changeword` is recognized only with parameters.

Relaxing the lexical rules of m4 might be useful (for example) if you wanted to apply translations to a file of numbers:

```
ifdef(`changeword', `', `errprint(` skipping: no changeword support
')m4exit(`77')')dnl
changeword(`[_a-zA-Z0-9]+')
⇒
define(`1', `0')1
⇒0
```

Tightening the lexical rules is less useful, because it will generally make some of the builtins unavailable. You could use it to prevent accidental call of builtins, for example:

```
ifdef(`changeword', `', `errprint(` skipping: no changeword support
')m4exit(`77')')dnl
define(`_indir', defn(`indir'))
⇒
changeword(`_[_a-zA-Z0-9]*')
⇒
esyscmd(`foo')
⇒esyscmd(foo)
_indir(`esyscmd', `echo hi')
⇒hi
⇒
```

Because m4 constructs its words a character at a time, there is a restriction on the regular expressions that may be passed to `changeword`. This is that if your regular expression accepts 'foo', it must also accept 'f' and 'fo'.

```
ifdef(`changeword', `', `errprint(` skipping: no changeword support
')m4exit(`77')')dnl
define(`foo
', `bar
')
⇒
dnl This example wants to recognize changeword, dnl, and `foo\n'.
dnl First, we check that our regexp will match.
regexp(`changeword', `[cd][a-z]*\|foo[
]')
⇒0
regexp(`foo
', `[cd][a-z]*\|foo[
]')
⇒0
regexp(`f', `[cd][a-z]*\|foo[
]')
⇒-1
foo
```

```
⇒foo
changeword('[cd][a-z]*\|foo[
]')
⇒
dnl Even though 'foo\n' matches, we forgot to allow 'f'.
foo
⇒foo
changeword('[cd][a-z]*\|fo*[
]?')
⇒
dnl Now we can call 'foo\n'.
foo
⇒bar
```

changeword has another function. If the regular expression supplied contains any grouped subexpressions, then text outside the first of these is discarded before symbol lookup. So:

```
ifdef('changeword', '', 'errprint(' skipping: no changeword support
')m4exit('77')')dnl
ifdef('__unix__', ,
        'errprint(' skipping: syscmd does not have unix semantics
')m4exit('77')')dnl
changecom('/*', '*/')dnl
define('foo', 'bar')dnl
changeword('#\([_a-zA-Z0-9]*\)')
⇒
#esyscmd('echo foo \#foo')
⇒foo bar
⇒
```

m4 now requires a '#' mark at the beginning of every macro invocation, so one can use m4 to preprocess plain text without losing various words like 'divert'.

In m4, macro substitution is based on text, while in TeX, it is based on tokens. changeword can throw this difference into relief. For example, here is the same idea represented in TeX and m4. First, the TeX version:

```
\def\a{\message{Hello}}
\catcode'\@=0
\catcode'\\=12
@a
@bye
⇒Hello
```

Then, the m4 version:

```
ifdef('changeword', '', 'errprint(' skipping: no changeword support
')m4exit('77')')dnl
define('a', 'errprint('Hello')')dnl
changeword('@\([_a-zA-Z0-9]*\)')
⇒
```

```
@a
⇒errprint(Hello)
```

In the TEX example, the first line defines a macro **a** to print the message 'Hello'. The second line defines @ to be usable instead of \ as an escape character. The third line defines \ to be a normal printing character, not an escape. The fourth line invokes the macro **a**. So, when TEX is run on this file, it displays the message 'Hello'.

When the **m4** example is passed through **m4**, it outputs 'errprint(Hello)'. The reason for this is that TEX does lexical analysis of macro definition when the macro is *defined*. **m4** just stores the text, postponing the lexical analysis until the macro is *used*.

You should note that using **changeword** will slow **m4** down by a factor of about seven, once it is changed to something other than the default regular expression. You can invoke **changeword** with the empty string to restore the default word definition, and regain the parsing speed.

8.5 Saving text until end of input

It is possible to 'save' some text until the end of the normal input has been seen. Text can be saved, to be read again by **m4** when the normal input has been exhausted. This feature is normally used to initiate cleanup actions before normal exit, e.g., deleting temporary files.

To save input text, use the builtin **m4wrap**:

m4wrap (*string*, ...)   [Builtin]
    Stores *string* in a safe place, to be reread when end of input is reached. As a GNU extension, additional arguments are concatenated with a space to the *string*.

    The expansion of **m4wrap** is void. The macro **m4wrap** is recognized only with parameters.

```
define('cleanup', 'This is the 'cleanup' action.
')
⇒
m4wrap('cleanup')
⇒
This is the first and last normal input line.
⇒This is the first and last normal input line.
^D
⇒This is the cleanup action.
```

The saved input is only reread when the end of normal input is seen, and not if **m4exit** is used to exit **m4**.

It is safe to call **m4wrap** from saved text, but then the order in which the saved text is reread is undefined. If **m4wrap** is not used recursively, the saved pieces of text are reread in the opposite order in which they were saved (LIFO—last in, first out). However, this behavior is likely to change in a future release, to match POSIX, so you should not depend on this order.

It is possible to emulate POSIX behavior even with older versions of GNU M4 by including the file **m4-1.4.17/examples/wrapfifo.m4** from the distribution:

```
$ m4 -I examples
undivert('wrapfifo.m4')dnl
⇒dnl Redefine m4wrap to have FIFO semantics.
⇒define('_m4wrap_level', '0')dnl
⇒define('m4wrap',
⇒'ifdef('m4wrap'_m4wrap_level,
⇒        'define('m4wrap'_m4wrap_level,
⇒                defn('m4wrap'_m4wrap_level)'$1')',
⇒        'builtin('m4wrap', 'define('_m4wrap_level',
⇒                                incr(_m4wrap_level))dnl
⇒m4wrap'_m4wrap_level)dnl
⇒define('m4wrap'_m4wrap_level, '$1')')')dnl
include('wrapfifo.m4')
⇒
m4wrap('a''m4wrap('c
', 'd')')m4wrap('b')
⇒
^D
⇒abc
```

It is likewise possible to emulate LIFO behavior without resorting to the GNU M4 extension of `builtin`, by including the file `m4-1.4.17/examples/wraplifo.m4` from the distribution. (Unfortunately, both examples shown here share some subtle bugs. See if you can find and correct them; or see Section 17.5 [Answers], page 125).

```
$ m4 -I examples
undivert('wraplifo.m4')dnl
⇒dnl Redefine m4wrap to have LIFO semantics.
⇒define('_m4wrap_level', '0')dnl
⇒define('_m4wrap', defn('m4wrap'))dnl
⇒define('m4wrap',
⇒'ifdef('m4wrap'_m4wrap_level,
⇒        'define('m4wrap'_m4wrap_level,
⇒                '$1'defn('m4wrap'_m4wrap_level))',
⇒        '_m4wrap('define('_m4wrap_level', incr(_m4wrap_level))dnl
⇒m4wrap'_m4wrap_level)dnl
⇒define('m4wrap'_m4wrap_level, '$1')')')dnl
include('wraplifo.m4')
⇒
m4wrap('a''m4wrap('c
', 'd')')m4wrap('b')
⇒
^D
⇒bac
```

Here is an example of implementing a factorial function using `m4wrap`:

```
define('f', 'ifelse('$1', '0', 'Answer: 0!=1
', eval('$1>1')), '0', 'Answer: $2$1=eval('$2$1')
', 'm4wrap('f(decr('$1'), '$2$1*')')')')
```

```
⇒
f('10')
⇒
^D
⇒Answer: 10*9*8*7*6*5*4*3*2*1=3628800
```

Invocations of m4wrap at the same recursion level are concatenated and rescanned as usual:

```
define('aa', 'AA
')
⇒
m4wrap('a')m4wrap('a')
⇒
^D
⇒AA
```

however, the transition between recursion levels behaves like an end of file condition between two input files.

```
m4wrap('m4wrap(')')len(abc')
⇒
^D
error m4:stdin:1: ERROR: end of file in argument list
```

9 File inclusion

m4 allows you to include named files at any point in the input.

9.1 Including named files

There are two builtin macros in m4 for including files:

include (*file*)   [Builtin]
sinclude (*file*)   [Builtin]
>   Both macros cause the file named *file* to be read by m4. When the end of the file is
>   reached, input is resumed from the previous input file.
>
>   The expansion of include and sinclude is therefore the contents of *file*.
>
>   If *file* does not exist, is a directory, or cannot otherwise be read, the expansion is
>   void, and include will fail with an error while sinclude is silent. The empty string
>   counts as a file that does not exist.
>
>   The macros include and sinclude are recognized only with parameters.
>
>    ```
>    include('none')
>    ```
>   `error` m4:stdin:1: cannot open 'none': No such file or directory
>   ⇒
>    ```
>    include()
>    ```
>   `error` m4:stdin:2: cannot open '': No such file or directory
>   ⇒
>    ```
>    sinclude('none')
>    ⇒
>    sinclude()
>    ⇒
>    ```

The rest of this section assumes that m4 is invoked with the -I option (see Section 2.2
[Invoking m4], page 8) pointing to the m4-1.4.17/examples directory shipped as part of
the GNU m4 package. The file m4-1.4.17/examples/incl.m4 in the distribution contains
the lines:

```
$ cat examples/incl.m4
⇒Include file start
⇒foo
⇒Include file end
```

Normally file inclusion is used to insert the contents of a file into the input stream. The
contents of the file will be read by m4 and macro calls in the file will be expanded:

```
$ m4 -I examples
define('foo', 'FOO')
⇒
include('incl.m4')
⇒Include file start
⇒FOO
⇒Include file end
⇒
```

The fact that `include` and `sinclude` expand to the contents of the file can be used to define macros that operate on entire files. Here is an example, which defines 'bar' to expand to the contents of `incl.m4`:

```
$ m4 -I examples
define('bar', include('incl.m4'))
⇒
This is 'bar':  >>bar<<
⇒This is bar:  >>Include file start
⇒foo
⇒Include file end
⇒<<
```

This use of `include` is not trivial, though, as files can contain quotes, commas, and parentheses, which can interfere with the way the `m4` parser works. GNU `m4` seamlessly concatenates the file contents with the next character, even if the included file ended in the middle of a comment, string, or macro call. These conditions are only treated as end of file errors if specified as input files on the command line.

In GNU `m4`, an alternative method of reading files is using `undivert` (see Section 10.2 [Undivert], page 76) on a named file.

9.2 Searching for include files

GNU `m4` allows included files to be found in other directories than the current working directory.

If the `--prepend-include` or `-B` command-line option was provided (see Section 2.2 [Invoking m4], page 8), those directories are searched first, in reverse order that those options were listed on the command line. Then `m4` looks in the current working directory. Next comes the directories specified with the `--include` or `-I` option, in the order found on the command line. Finally, if the `M4PATH` environment variable is set, it is expected to contain a colon-separated list of directories, which will be searched in order.

If the automatic search for include-files causes trouble, the 'p' debug flag (see Section 7.3 [Debug Levels], page 58) can help isolate the problem.

10 Diverting and undiverting output

Diversions are a way of temporarily saving output. The output of m4 can at any time be diverted to a temporary file, and be reinserted into the output stream, *undiverted*, again at a later time.

Numbered diversions are counted from 0 upwards, diversion number 0 being the normal output stream. GNU m4 tries to keep diversions in memory. However, there is a limit to the overall memory usable by all diversions taken together (512K, currently). When this maximum is about to be exceeded, a temporary file is opened to receive the contents of the biggest diversion still in memory, freeing this memory for other diversions. When creating the temporary file, m4 honors the value of the environment variable TMPDIR, and falls back to /tmp. Thus, the amount of available disk space provides the only real limit on the number and aggregate size of diversions.

Diversions make it possible to generate output in a different order than the input was read. It is possible to implement topological sorting dependencies. For example, GNU Autoconf makes use of diversions under the hood to ensure that the expansion of a prerequisite macro appears in the output prior to the expansion of a dependent macro, regardless of which order the two macros were invoked in the user's input file.

10.1 Diverting output

Output is diverted using divert:

divert ([*number* = '0'])   [Builtin]
> The current diversion is changed to *number*. If *number* is left out or empty, it is assumed to be zero. If *number* cannot be parsed, the diversion is unchanged.
>
> The expansion of divert is void.

When all the m4 input will have been processed, all existing diversions are automatically undiverted, in numerical order.

```
divert('1')
This text is diverted.
divert
⇒
This text is not diverted.
⇒This text is not diverted.
^D
⇒
⇒This text is diverted.
```

Several calls of divert with the same argument do not overwrite the previous diverted text, but append to it. Diversions are printed after any wrapped text is expanded.

```
define('text', 'TEXT')
⇒
divert('1')'diverted text.'
divert
⇒
```

```
m4wrap('Wrapped text precedes ')
⇒
^D
⇒Wrapped TEXT precedes diverted text.
```

If output is diverted to a negative diversion, it is simply discarded. This can be used to suppress unwanted output. A common example of unwanted output is the trailing newlines after macro definitions. Here is a common programming idiom in m4 for avoiding them.

```
divert('-1')
define('foo', 'Macro 'foo'.')
define('bar', 'Macro 'bar'.')
divert
⇒
```

Traditional implementations only supported ten diversions. But as a GNU extension, diversion numbers can be as large as positive integers will allow, rather than treating a multi-digit diversion number as a request to discard text.

```
divert(eval('1<<28'))world
divert('2')hello
^D
⇒hello
⇒world
```

Note that divert is an English word, but also an active macro without arguments. When processing plain text, the word might appear in normal text and be unintentionally swallowed as a macro invocation. One way to avoid this is to use the -P option to rename all builtins (see Section 2.1 [Invoking m4], page 7). Another is to write a wrapper that requires a parameter to be recognized.

```
We decided to divert the stream for irrigation.
⇒We decided to  the stream for irrigation.
define('divert', 'ifelse('$#', '0', ''$0'', 'builtin('$0', $@)')')
⇒
divert('-1')
Ignored text.
divert('0')
⇒
We decided to divert the stream for irrigation.
⇒We decided to divert the stream for irrigation.
```

10.2 Undiverting output

Diverted text can be undiverted explicitly using the builtin undivert:

undivert ([*diversions...*])   [Builtin]
Undiverts the numeric *diversions* given by the arguments, in the order given. If no arguments are supplied, all diversions are undiverted, in numerical order.

As a GNU extension, *diversions* may contain non-numeric strings, which are treated as the names of files to copy into the output without expansion. A warning is issued if a file could not be opened.

The expansion of `undivert` is void.

```
divert('1')
This text is diverted.
divert
⇒
This text is not diverted.
⇒This text is not diverted.
undivert('1')
⇒
⇒This text is diverted.
⇒
```

Notice the last two blank lines. One of them comes from the newline following `undivert`, the other from the newline that followed the `divert`! A diversion often starts with a blank line like this.

When diverted text is undiverted, it is *not* reread by m4, but rather copied directly to the current output, and it is therefore not an error to undivert into a diversion. Undiverting the empty string is the same as specifying diversion 0; in either case nothing happens since the output has already been flushed.

```
divert('1')diverted text
divert
⇒
undivert()
⇒
undivert('0')
⇒
undivert
⇒diverted text
⇒
divert('1')more
divert('2')undivert('1')diverted text''divert
⇒
undivert('1')
⇒
undivert('2')
⇒more
⇒diverted text
```

When a diversion has been undiverted, the diverted text is discarded, and it is not possible to bring back diverted text more than once.

```
divert('1')
This text is diverted first.
divert('0')undivert('1')dnl
⇒
⇒This text is diverted first.
undivert('1')
⇒
```

```
divert('1')
This text is also diverted but not appended.
divert('0')undivert('1')dnl
⇒
⇒This text is also diverted but not appended.
```

Attempts to undivert the current diversion are silently ignored. Thus, when the current diversion is not 0, the current diversion does not get rearranged among the other diversions.

```
divert('1')one
divert('2')two
divert('3')three
divert('2')undivert''dnl
divert''undivert''dnl
⇒two
⇒one
⇒three
```

GNU `m4` allows named files to be undiverted. Given a non-numeric argument, the contents of the file named will be copied, uninterpreted, to the current output. This complements the builtin `include` (see Section 9.1 [Include], page 73). To illustrate the difference, assume the file `foo` contains:

```
$ cat foo
bar
```

then

```
define('bar', 'BAR')
⇒
undivert('foo')
⇒bar
⇒
include('foo')
⇒BAR
⇒
```

If the file is not found (or cannot be read), an error message is issued, and the expansion is void. It is possible to intermix files and diversion numbers.

```
divert('1')diversion one
divert('2')undivert('foo')dnl
divert('3')diversion three
divert''dnl
undivert('1', '2', 'foo', '3')dnl
⇒diversion one
⇒bar
⇒bar
⇒diversion three
```

10.3 Diversion numbers

The current diversion is tracked by the builtin `divnum`:

divnum   [Builtin]

> Expands to the number of the current diversion.

```
Initial divnum
⇒Initial 0
divert('1')
Diversion one: divnum
divert('2')
Diversion two: divnum
^D
⇒
⇒Diversion one: 1
⇒
⇒Diversion two: 2
```

10.4 Discarding diverted text

Often it is not known, when output is diverted, whether the diverted text is actually needed. Since all non-empty diversion are brought back on the main output stream when the end of input is seen, a method of discarding a diversion is needed. If all diversions should be discarded, the easiest is to end the input to m4 with 'divert('-1')' followed by an explicit 'undivert':

```
divert('1')
Diversion one: divnum
divert('2')
Diversion two: divnum
divert('-1')
undivert
^D
```

No output is produced at all.

Clearing selected diversions can be done with the following macro:

cleardivert ([*diversions...*])   [Composite]

> Discard the contents of each of the listed numeric *diversions*.

```
define('cleardivert',
'pushdef('_n', divnum)divert('-1')undivert($@)divert(_n)popdef('_n')')
⇒
```

It is called just like undivert, but the effect is to clear the diversions, given by the arguments. (This macro has a nasty bug! You should try to see if you can find it and correct it; or see Section 17.6 [Answers], page 126).

11 Macros for text handling

There are a number of builtins in `m4` for manipulating text in various ways, extracting substrings, searching, substituting, and so on.

11.1 Calculating length of strings

The length of a string can be calculated by `len`:

len (*string*)   [Builtin]
> Expands to the length of *string*, as a decimal number.
>
> The macro `len` is recognized only with parameters.
>
> ```
> len()
> ⇒0
> len(`abcdef')
> ⇒6
> ```

11.2 Searching for substrings

Searching for substrings is done with `index`:

index (*string*, *substring*)   [Builtin]
> Expands to the index of the first occurrence of *substring* in *string*. The first character in *string* has index 0. If *substring* does not occur in *string*, `index` expands to '`-1`'.
>
> The macro `index` is recognized only with parameters.
>
> ```
> index(`gnus, gnats, and armadillos', `nat')
> ⇒7
> index(`gnus, gnats, and armadillos', `dag')
> ⇒-1
> ```

Omitting *substring* evokes a warning, but still produces output; contrast this with an empty *substring*.

> ```
> index(`abc')
> error m4:stdin:1: Warning: too few arguments to builtin `index'
> ⇒0
> index(`abc', `')
> ⇒0
> index(`abc', `b')
> ⇒1
> ```

11.3 Searching for regular expressions

Searching for regular expressions is done with the builtin `regexp`:

regexp (*string*, *regexp*, [*replacement*])   [Builtin]
> Searches for *regexp* in *string*. The syntax for regular expressions is the same as in GNU Emacs, which is similar to BRE, Basic Regular Expressions in POSIX. See Section "Syntax of Regular Expressions" in *The GNU Emacs Manual*. Support for

ERE, Extended Regular Expressions is not available, but will be added in GNU M4 2.0.

If *replacement* is omitted, `regexp` expands to the index of the first match of *regexp* in *string*. If *regexp* does not match anywhere in *string*, it expands to -1.

If *replacement* is supplied, and there was a match, `regexp` changes the expansion to this argument, with '\n' substituted by the text matched by the *n*th parenthesized sub-expression of *regexp*, up to nine sub-expressions. The escape '\&' is replaced by the text of the entire regular expression matched. For all other characters, '\' treats the next character literally. A warning is issued if there were fewer sub-expressions than the '\n' requested, or if there is a trailing '\'. If there was no match, `regexp` expands to the empty string.

The macro `regexp` is recognized only with parameters.

```
regexp('GNUs not Unix', '\<[a-z]\w+')
⇒5
regexp('GNUs not Unix', '\<Q\w*')
⇒-1
regexp('GNUs not Unix', '\w\(\w+\)$', '*** \& *** \1 ***')
⇒*** Unix *** nix ***
regexp('GNUs not Unix', '\<Q\w*', '*** \& *** \1 ***')
⇒
```

Here are some more examples on the handling of backslash:

```
regexp('abc', '\(b\)', '\\\10\a')
⇒\b0a
regexp('abc', 'b', '\1\')
error  m4:stdin:2: Warning: sub-expression 1 not present
error  m4:stdin:2: Warning: trailing \ ignored in replacement
⇒
regexp('abc', '\(\(d\)?\)\(c\)', '\1\2\3\4\5\6')
error  m4:stdin:3: Warning: sub-expression 4 not present
error  m4:stdin:3: Warning: sub-expression 5 not present
error  m4:stdin:3: Warning: sub-expression 6 not present
⇒c
```

Omitting *regexp* evokes a warning, but still produces output; contrast this with an empty *regexp* argument.

```
regexp('abc')
error  m4:stdin:1: Warning: too few arguments to builtin 'regexp'
⇒0
regexp('abc', '')
⇒0
regexp('abc', '', '\\def')
⇒\def
```

11.4 Extracting substrings

Substrings are extracted with `substr`:

substr (*string*, *from*, [*length*])   [Builtin]

Expands to the substring of *string*, which starts at index *from*, and extends for *length* characters, or to the end of *string*, if *length* is omitted. The starting index of a string is always 0. The expansion is empty if there is an error parsing *from* or *length*, if *from* is beyond the end of *string*, or if *length* is negative.

The macro `substr` is recognized only with parameters.

```
substr('gnus, gnats, and armadillos', '6')
⇒gnats, and armadillos
substr('gnus, gnats, and armadillos', '6', '5')
⇒gnats
```

Omitting *from* evokes a warning, but still produces output.

```
substr('abc')
error m4:stdin:1: Warning: too few arguments to builtin 'substr'
⇒abc
substr('abc',)
error m4:stdin:2: empty string treated as 0 in builtin 'substr'
⇒abc
```

11.5 Translating characters

Character translation is done with `translit`:

translit (*string*, *chars*, [*replacement*])   [Builtin]

Expands to *string*, with each character that occurs in *chars* translated into the character from *replacement* with the same index.

If *replacement* is shorter than *chars*, the excess characters of *chars* are deleted from the expansion; if *chars* is shorter, the excess characters in *replacement* are silently ignored. If *replacement* is omitted, all characters in *string* that are present in *chars* are deleted from the expansion. If a character appears more than once in *chars*, only the first instance is used in making the translation. Only a single translation pass is made, even if characters in *replacement* also appear in *chars*.

As a GNU extension, both *chars* and *replacement* can contain character-ranges, e.g., 'a-z' (meaning all lowercase letters) or '0-9' (meaning all digits). To include a dash '-' in *chars* or *replacement*, place it first or last in the entire string, or as the last character of a range. Back-to-back ranges can share a common endpoint. It is not an error for the last character in the range to be 'larger' than the first. In that case, the range runs backwards, i.e., '9-0' means the string '9876543210'. The expansion of a range is dependent on the underlying encoding of characters, so using ranges is not always portable between machines.

The macro `translit` is recognized only with parameters.

```
translit('GNUs not Unix', 'A-Z')
⇒s not nix
translit('GNUs not Unix', 'a-z', 'A-Z')
⇒GNUS NOT UNIX
translit('GNUs not Unix', 'A-Z', 'z-a')
```

```
⇒tmfs not fnix
translit('+,-12345', '+--1-5', '<;>a-c-a')
⇒<;>abcba
translit('abcdef', 'aabdef', 'bcged')
⇒bgced
```

In the ASCII encoding, the first example deletes all uppercase letters, the second converts lowercase to uppercase, and the third 'mirrors' all uppercase letters, while converting them to lowercase. The two first cases are by far the most common, even though they are not portable to EBCDIC or other encodings. The fourth example shows a range ending in '-', as well as back-to-back ranges. The final example shows that 'a' is mapped to 'b', not 'c'; the resulting 'b' is not further remapped to 'g'; the 'd' and 'e' are swapped, and the 'f' is discarded.

Omitting *chars* evokes a warning, but still produces output.

```
translit('abc')
error m4:stdin:1: Warning: too few arguments to builtin 'translit'
⇒abc
```

11.6 Substituting text by regular expression

Global substitution in a string is done by patsubst:

patsubst (*string*, *regexp*, [*replacement*])   [Builtin]

Searches *string* for matches of *regexp*, and substitutes *replacement* for each match. The syntax for regular expressions is the same as in GNU Emacs (see Section 11.3 [Regexp], page 81).

The parts of *string* that are not covered by any match of *regexp* are copied to the expansion. Whenever a match is found, the search proceeds from the end of the match, so a character from *string* will never be substituted twice. If *regexp* matches a string of zero length, the start position for the search is incremented, to avoid infinite loops.

When a replacement is to be made, *replacement* is inserted into the expansion, with '\n' substituted by the text matched by the nth parenthesized sub-expression of *patsubst*, for up to nine sub-expressions. The escape '\&' is replaced by the text of the entire regular expression matched. For all other characters, '\' treats the next character literally. A warning is issued if there were fewer sub-expressions than the '\n' requested, or if there is a trailing '\'.

The *replacement* argument can be omitted, in which case the text matched by *regexp* is deleted.

The macro patsubst is recognized only with parameters.

```
patsubst('GNUs not Unix', '^', 'OBS: ')
⇒OBS: GNUs not Unix
patsubst('GNUs not Unix', '\<', 'OBS: ')
⇒OBS: GNUs OBS: not OBS: Unix
patsubst('GNUs not Unix', '\w*', '(\&)')
⇒(GNUs)() (not)() (Unix)()
patsubst('GNUs not Unix', '\w+', '(\&)')
```

```
⇒(GNUs) (not) (Unix)
patsubst('GNUs not Unix', '[A-Z][a-z]+')
⇒GN not
patsubst('GNUs not Unix', 'not', 'NOT\')
```
error m4:stdin:6: Warning: trailing \ ignored in replacement
```
⇒GNUs NOT Unix
```

Here is a slightly more realistic example, which capitalizes individual words or whole sentences, by substituting calls of the macros **upcase** and **downcase** into the strings.

upcase (*text*)   [Composite]
downcase (*text*)   [Composite]
capitalize (*text*)   [Composite]

Expand to *text*, but with capitalization changed: **upcase** changes all letters to upper case, **downcase** changes all letters to lower case, and **capitalize** changes the first character of each word to upper case and the remaining characters to lower case.

First, an example of their usage, using implementations distributed in `m4-1.4.17/examples/capitalize.m4`.

```
$ m4 -I examples
include('capitalize.m4')
⇒
upcase('GNUs not Unix')
⇒GNUS NOT UNIX
downcase('GNUs not Unix')
⇒gnus not unix
capitalize('GNUs not Unix')
⇒Gnus Not Unix
```

Now for the implementation. There is a helper macro **_capitalize** which puts only its first word in mixed case. Then **capitalize** merely parses out the words, and replaces them with an invocation of **_capitalize**. (As presented here, the **capitalize** macro has some subtle flaws. You should try to see if you can find and correct them; or see Section 17.7 [Answers], page 127).

```
$ m4 -I examples
undivert('capitalize.m4')dnl
⇒divert('-1')
⇒# upcase(text)
⇒# downcase(text)
⇒# capitalize(text)
⇒#   change case of text, simple version
⇒define('upcase', 'translit('$*', 'a-z', 'A-Z')')
⇒define('downcase', 'translit('$*', 'A-Z', 'a-z')')
⇒define('_capitalize',
⇒        'regexp('$1', '^\(\w\)\(\w*\)',
⇒                'upcase('\1')''downcase('\2')')')
⇒define('capitalize', 'patsubst('$1', '\w+', '_$0('\&')')')
⇒divert''dnl
```

While `regexp` replaces the whole input with the replacement as soon as there is a match, `patsubst` replaces each *occurrence* of a match and preserves non-matching pieces:

```
define('patreg',
'patsubst($@)
regexp($@)')dnl
patreg('bar foo baz Foo', 'foo\|Foo', 'FOO')
⇒bar FOO baz FOO
⇒FOO
patreg('aba abb 121', '\(.\)\(.\)\1', '\2\1\2')
⇒bab abb 212
⇒bab
```

Omitting *regexp* evokes a warning, but still produces output; contrast this with an empty *regexp* argument.

```
patsubst('abc')
error m4:stdin:1: Warning: too few arguments to builtin 'patsubst'
⇒abc
patsubst('abc', '')
⇒abc
patsubst('abc', '', '\\-')
⇒\-a\-b\-c\-
```

11.7 Formatting strings (printf-like)

Formatted output can be made with `format`:

format (*format-string*, ...)   [Builtin]
    Works much like the C function `printf`. The first argument *format-string* can contain '%' specifications which are satisfied by additional arguments, and the expansion of `format` is the formatted string.

    The macro `format` is recognized only with parameters.

Its use is best described by a few examples:

```
define('foo', 'The brown fox jumped over the lazy dog')
⇒
format('The string "%s" uses %d characters', foo, len(foo))
⇒The string "The brown fox jumped over the lazy dog" uses 38 characters
format('%*.*d', '-1', '-1', '1')
⇒1
format('%.0f', '56789.9876')
⇒56790
len(format('%-*X', '5000', '1'))
⇒5000
ifelse(format('%010F', 'infinity'), '       INF', 'success',
       format('%010F', 'infinity'), '  INFINITY', 'success',
       format('%010F', 'infinity'))
⇒success
ifelse(format('%.1A', '1.999'), '0X1.0P+1', 'success',
```

```
          format('%.1A', '1.999'), '0X2.0P+0', 'success',
          format('%.1A', '1.999'))
⇒success
format('%g', '0xa.P+1')
⇒20
```

Using the `forloop` macro defined earlier (see Section 6.4 [Forloop], page 46), this example shows how `format` can be used to produce tabular output.

```
$ m4 -I examples
include('forloop.m4')
⇒
forloop('i', '1', '10', 'format('%6d squared is %10d
', i, eval(i**2))')
⇒       1 squared is          1
⇒       2 squared is          4
⇒       3 squared is          9
⇒       4 squared is         16
⇒       5 squared is         25
⇒       6 squared is         36
⇒       7 squared is         49
⇒       8 squared is         64
⇒       9 squared is         81
⇒      10 squared is        100
⇒
```

The builtin `format` is modeled after the ANSI C 'printf' function, and supports these '%' specifiers: 'c', 's', 'd', 'o', 'x', 'X', 'u', 'a', 'A', 'e', 'E', 'f', 'F', 'g', 'G', and '%'; it supports field widths and precisions, and the flags '+', '-', ' ', '0', '#', and '''. For integer specifiers, the width modifiers 'hh', 'h', and 'l' are recognized, and for floating point specifiers, the width modifier 'l' is recognized. Items not yet supported include positional arguments, the 'n', 'p', 'S', and 'C' specifiers, the 'z', 't', 'j', 'L' and 'll' modifiers, and any platform extensions available in the native `printf`. For more details on the functioning of `printf`, see the C Library Manual, or the POSIX specification (for example, '%a' is supported even on platforms that haven't yet implemented C99 hexadecimal floating point output natively).

Unrecognized specifiers result in a warning. It is anticipated that a future release of GNU `m4` will support more specifiers, and give better warnings when various problems such as overflow are encountered. Likewise, escape sequences are not yet recognized.

```
format('%p', '0')
error m4:stdin:1: Warning: unrecognized specifier in '%p'
⇒
```

12 Macros for doing arithmetic

Integer arithmetic is included in m4, with a C-like syntax. As convenient shorthands, there are builtins for simple increment and decrement operations.

12.1 Decrement and increment operators

Increment and decrement of integers are supported using the builtins incr and decr:

incr (*number*)   [Builtin]
decr (*number*)   [Builtin]
> Expand to the numerical value of *number*, incremented or decremented, respectively, by one. Except for the empty string, the expansion is empty if *number* could not be parsed.
>
> The macros incr and decr are recognized only with parameters.

```
incr(`4')
⇒5
decr(`7')
⇒6
incr()
error m4:stdin:3: empty string treated as 0 in builtin `incr'
⇒1
decr()
error m4:stdin:4: empty string treated as 0 in builtin `decr'
⇒-1
```

12.2 Evaluating integer expressions

Integer expressions are evaluated with eval:

eval (*expression*, [*radix* = `10'], [*width*])   [Builtin]
> Expands to the value of *expression*. The expansion is empty if a problem is encountered while parsing the arguments. If specified, *radix* and *width* control the format of the output.
>
> Calculations are done with 32-bit signed numbers. Overflow silently results in wraparound. A warning is issued if division by zero is attempted, or if *expression* could not be parsed.
>
> Expressions can contain the following operators, listed in order of decreasing precedence.

`()'	Parentheses
`+ - ~ !'	Unary plus and minus, and bitwise and logical negation
`**'	Exponentiation
`* / %'	Multiplication, division, and modulo
`+ -'	Addition and subtraction
`<< >>'	Shift left or right

'> >= < <='
                    Relational operators

'== !='   Equality operators

'&'   Bitwise and

'^'   Bitwise exclusive-or

'|'   Bitwise or

'&&'   Logical and

'||'   Logical or

The macro `eval` is recognized only with parameters.

All binary operators, except exponentiation, are left associative. C operators that perform variable assignment, such as '+=' or '--', are not implemented, since `eval` only operates on constants, not variables. Attempting to use them results in an error. However, since traditional implementations treated '=' as an undocumented alias for '==' as opposed to an assignment operator, this usage is supported as a special case. Be aware that a future version of GNU M4 may support assignment semantics as an extension when POSIX mode is not requested, and that using '=' to check equality is not portable.

```
eval('2 = 2')
error m4:stdin:1: Warning: recommend ==, not =, for equality operator
⇒1
eval('++0')
error m4:stdin:2: invalid operator in eval: ++0
⇒
eval('0 |= 1')
error m4:stdin:3: invalid operator in eval: 0 |= 1
⇒
```

Note that some older `m4` implementations use '^' as an alternate operator for the exponentiation, although POSIX requires the C behavior of bitwise exclusive-or. The precedence of the negation operators, '~' and '!', was traditionally lower than equality. The unary operators could not be used reliably more than once on the same term without intervening parentheses. The traditional precedence of the equality operators '==' and '!=' was identical instead of lower than the relational operators such as '<', even through GNU M4 1.4.8. Starting with version 1.4.9, GNU M4 correctly follows POSIX precedence rules. M4 scripts designed to be portable between releases must be aware that parentheses may be required to enforce C precedence rules. Likewise, division by zero, even in the unused branch of a short-circuiting operator, is not always well-defined in other implementations.

Following are some examples where the current version of M4 follows C precedence rules, but where older versions and some other implementations of `m4` require explicit parentheses to get the correct result:

```
eval('1 == 2 > 0')
⇒1
eval('(1 == 2) > 0')
⇒0
```

```
eval('! 0 * 2')
⇒2
eval('! (0 * 2)')
⇒1
eval('1 | 1 ^ 1')
⇒1
eval('(1 | 1) ^ 1')
⇒0
eval('+ + - ~ ! ~ 0')
⇒1
eval('2 || 1 / 0')
⇒1
eval('0 || 1 / 0')
error m4:stdin:9: divide by zero in eval: 0 || 1 / 0
⇒
eval('0 && 1 % 0')
⇒0
eval('2 && 1 % 0')
error m4:stdin:11: modulo by zero in eval: 2 && 1 % 0
⇒
```

As a GNU extension, the operator '**' performs integral exponentiation. The operator is right-associative, and if evaluated, the exponent must be non-negative, and at least one of the arguments must be non-zero, or a warning is issued.

```
eval('2 ** 3 ** 2')
⇒512
eval('(2 ** 3) ** 2')
⇒64
eval('0 ** 1')
⇒0
eval('2 ** 0')
⇒1
eval('0 ** 0')
⇒
error m4:stdin:5: divide by zero in eval: 0 ** 0
eval('4 ** -2')
error m4:stdin:6: negative exponent in eval: 4 ** -2
⇒
```

Within *expression*, (but not *radix* or *width*), numbers without a special prefix are decimal. A simple '0' prefix introduces an octal number. '0x' introduces a hexadecimal number. As GNU extensions, '0b' introduces a binary number. '0r' introduces a number expressed in any radix between 1 and 36: the prefix should be immediately followed by the decimal expression of the radix, a colon, then the digits making the number. For radix 1, leading zeros are ignored, and all remaining digits must be '1'; for all other radices, the digits are '0', '1', '2', ... Beyond '9', the digits are 'a', 'b' ... up to 'z'. Lower and upper case letters can be used interchangeably in numbers prefixes and as number digits.

Parentheses may be used to group subexpressions whenever needed. For the relational operators, a true relation returns 1, and a false relation return 0.

Here are a few examples of use of `eval`.

```
eval('-3 * 5')
⇒-15
eval('-99 / 10')
⇒-9
eval('-99 % 10')
⇒-9
eval('99 % -10')
⇒9
eval(index('Hello world', 'llo') >= 0)
⇒1
eval('0r1:0111 + 0b100 + 0r3:12')
⇒12
define('square', 'eval('($1) ** 2')')
⇒
square('9')
⇒81
square(square('5')' + 1')
⇒676
define('foo', '666')
⇒
eval('foo / 6')
 error  m4:stdin:11: bad expression in eval: foo / 6
⇒
eval(foo / 6)
⇒111
```

As the last two lines show, `eval` does not handle macro names, even if they expand to a valid expression (or part of a valid expression). Therefore all macros must be expanded before they are passed to `eval`.

Some calculations are not portable to other implementations, since they have undefined semantics in C, but GNU `m4` has well-defined behavior on overflow. When shifting, an out-of-range shift amount is implicitly brought into the range of 32-bit signed integers using an implicit bit-wise and with 0x1f).

```
define('max_int', eval('0x7fffffff'))
⇒
define('min_int', incr(max_int))
⇒
eval(min_int' < 0')
⇒1
eval(max_int' > 0')
⇒1
ifelse(eval(min_int' / -1'), min_int, 'overflow occurred')
⇒overflow occurred
min_int
```

```
⇒-2147483648
eval('0x80000000 % -1')
⇒0
eval('-4 >> 1')
⇒-2
eval('-4 >> 33')
⇒-2
```

If *radix* is specified, it specifies the radix to be used in the expansion. The default radix is 10; this is also the case if *radix* is the empty string. A warning results if the radix is outside the range of 1 through 36, inclusive. The result of eval is always taken to be signed. No radix prefix is output, and for radices greater than 10, the digits are lower case. The *width* argument specifies the minimum output width, excluding any negative sign. The result is zero-padded to extend the expansion to the requested width. A warning results if the width is negative. If *radix* or *width* is out of bounds, the expansion of eval is empty.

```
eval('666', '10')
⇒666
eval('666', '11')
⇒556
eval('666', '6')
⇒3030
eval('666', '6', '10')
⇒0000003030
eval('-666', '6', '10')
⇒-0000003030
eval('10', '', '0')
⇒10
'0r1:'eval('10', '1', '11')
⇒0r1:01111111111
eval('10', '16')
⇒a
eval('1', '37')
error m4:stdin:9: radix 37 in builtin 'eval' out of range
⇒
eval('1', , '-1')
error m4:stdin:10: negative width to builtin 'eval'
⇒
eval()
error m4:stdin:11: empty string treated as 0 in builtin 'eval'
⇒0
```

13 Macros for running shell commands

There are a few builtin macros in m4 that allow you to run shell commands from within m4.

Note that the definition of a valid shell command is system dependent. On UNIX systems, this is the typical /bin/sh. But on other systems, such as native Windows, the shell has a different syntax of commands that it understands. Some examples in this chapter assume /bin/sh, and also demonstrate how to quit early with a known exit value if this is not the case.

13.1 Determining the platform

Sometimes it is desirable for an input file to know which platform m4 is running on. GNU m4 provides several macros that are predefined to expand to the empty string; checking for their existence will confirm platform details.

__gnu__	[Optional builtin]
__os2__	[Optional builtin]
os2	[Optional builtin]
__unix__	[Optional builtin]
unix	[Optional builtin]
__windows__	[Optional builtin]
windows	[Optional builtin]

Each of these macros is conditionally defined as needed to describe the environment of m4. If defined, each macro expands to the empty string. For now, these macros silently ignore all arguments, but in a future release of M4, they might warn if arguments are present.

When GNU extensions are in effect (that is, when you did not use the -G option, see Section 2.3 [Invoking m4], page 10), GNU m4 will define the macro __gnu__ to expand to the empty string.

```
$ m4
__gnu__
⇒
__gnu__('ignored')
⇒
Extensions are ifdef('__gnu__', 'active', 'inactive')
⇒Extensions are active
$ m4 -G
__gnu__
⇒__gnu__
__gnu__('ignored')
⇒__gnu__(ignored)
Extensions are ifdef('__gnu__', 'active', 'inactive')
⇒Extensions are inactive
```

On UNIX systems, GNU m4 will define __unix__ by default, or unix when the -G option is specified.

On native Windows systems, GNU `m4` will define `__windows__` by default, or `windows` when the `-G` option is specified.

On OS/2 systems, GNU `m4` will define `__os2__` by default, or `os2` when the `-G` option is specified.

If GNU `m4` does not provide a platform macro for your system, please report that as a bug.

```
define('provided', '0')
⇒
ifdef('__unix__', 'define('provided', incr(provided))')
⇒
ifdef('__windows__', 'define('provided', incr(provided))')
⇒
ifdef('__os2__', 'define('provided', incr(provided))')
⇒
provided
⇒1
```

13.2 Executing simple commands

Any shell command can be executed, using `syscmd`:

syscmd (*shell-command*)   [Builtin]

Executes *shell-command* as a shell command.

The expansion of `syscmd` is void, *not* the output from *shell-command*! Output or error messages from *shell-command* are not read by `m4`. See Section 13.3 [Esyscmd], page 97, if you need to process the command output.

Prior to executing the command, `m4` flushes its buffers. The default standard input, output and error of *shell-command* are the same as those of `m4`.

By default, the *shell-command* will be used as the argument to the `-c` option of the `/bin/sh` shell (or the version of `sh` specified by 'command -p getconf PATH', if your system supports that). If you prefer a different shell, the `configure` script can be given the option `--with-syscmd-shell=`*location* to set the location of an alternative shell at GNU `m4` installation; the alternative shell must still support `-c`.

The macro `syscmd` is recognized only with parameters.

```
define('foo', 'FOO')
⇒
syscmd('echo foo')
⇒foo
⇒
```

Note how the expansion of `syscmd` keeps the trailing newline of the command, as well as using the newline that appeared after the macro.

The following is an example of *shell-command* using the same standard input as `m4`:

```
$ echo "m4wrap(\'syscmd(\'cat')')" | m4
⇒
```

It tells m4 to read all of its input before executing the wrapped text, then hand a valid (albeit emptied) pipe as standard input for the `cat` subcommand. Therefore, you should be careful when using standard input (either by specifying no files, or by passing '−' as a file name on the command line, see Section 2.6 [Invoking m4], page 12), and also invoking subcommands via `syscmd` or `esyscmd` that consume data from standard input. When standard input is a seekable file, the subprocess will pick up with the next character not yet processed by m4; when it is a pipe or other non-seekable file, there is no guarantee how much data will already be buffered by m4 and thus unavailable to the child.

13.3 Reading the output of commands

If you want m4 to read the output of a shell command, use `esyscmd`:

esyscmd (*shell-command*)   [Builtin]

>   Expands to the standard output of the shell command *shell-command*.
>
>   Prior to executing the command, m4 flushes its buffers. The default standard input and standard error of *shell-command* are the same as those of m4. The error output of *shell-command* is not a part of the expansion: it will appear along with the error output of m4.
>
>   By default, the *shell-command* will be used as the argument to the −c option of the `/bin/sh` shell (or the version of `sh` specified by 'command -p getconf PATH', if your system supports that). If you prefer a different shell, the `configure` script can be given the option `--with-syscmd-shell=location` to set the location of an alternative shell at GNU m4 installation; the alternative shell must still support −c.
>
>   The macro `esyscmd` is recognized only with parameters.
>
> ```
> define('foo', 'FOO')
> ⇒
> esyscmd('echo foo')
> ⇒FOO
> ⇒
> ```

Note how the expansion of `esyscmd` keeps the trailing newline of the command, as well as using the newline that appeared after the macro.

Just as with `syscmd`, care must be exercised when sharing standard input between m4 and the child process of `esyscmd`.

13.4 Exit status

To see whether a shell command succeeded, use `sysval`:

sysval   [Builtin]

>   Expands to the exit status of the last shell command run with `syscmd` or `esyscmd`. Expands to 0 if no command has been run yet.
>
> ```
> sysval
> ⇒0
> syscmd('false')
> ⇒
> ```

```
ifelse(sysval, `0', `zero', `non-zero')
⇒non-zero
syscmd(`exit 2')
⇒
sysval
⇒2
syscmd(`true')
⇒
sysval
⇒0
esyscmd(`false')
⇒
ifelse(sysval, `0', `zero', `non-zero')
⇒non-zero
esyscmd(`echo dnl && exit 127')
⇒
sysval
⇒127
esyscmd(`true')
⇒
sysval
⇒0
```

sysval results in 127 if there was a problem executing the command, for example, if the system-imposed argument length is exceeded, or if there were not enough resources to fork. It is not possible to distinguish between failed execution and successful execution that had an exit status of 127, unless there was output from the child process.

On UNIX platforms, where it is possible to detect when command execution is terminated by a signal, rather than a normal exit, the result is the signal number shifted left by eight bits.

```
dnl This test assumes kill is a shell builtin, and that signals are
dnl recognizable.
ifdef(`__unix__', ,
      `errprint(` skipping: syscmd does not have unix semantics
')m4exit(`77')')dnl
syscmd(`kill -9 $$')
⇒
sysval
⇒2304
syscmd()
⇒
sysval
⇒0
esyscmd(`kill -9 $$')
⇒
sysval
⇒2304
```

13.5 Making temporary files

Commands specified to `syscmd` or `esyscmd` might need a temporary file, for output or for some other purpose. There is a builtin macro, `mkstemp`, for making a temporary file:

`mkstemp (template)` [Builtin]
`maketemp (template)` [Builtin]

> Expands to the quoted name of a new, empty file, made from the string *template*, which should end with the string 'XXXXXX'. The six 'X' characters are then replaced with random characters matching the regular expression '[a-zA-Z0-9._-]', in order to make the file name unique. If fewer than six 'X' characters are found at the end of `template`, the result will be longer than the template. The created file will have access permissions as if by *chmod =rw,go=*, meaning that the current umask of the m4 process is taken into account, and at most only the current user can read and write the file.
>
> The traditional behavior, standardized by POSIX, is that `maketemp` merely replaces the trailing 'X' with the process id, without creating a file or quoting the expansion, and without ensuring that the resulting string is a unique file name. In part, this means that using the same *template* twice in the same input file will result in the same expansion. This behavior is a security hole, as it is very easy for another process to guess the name that will be generated, and thus interfere with a subsequent use of `syscmd` trying to manipulate that file name. Hence, POSIX has recommended that all new implementations of m4 provide the secure `mkstemp` builtin, and that users of m4 check for its existence.
>
> The expansion is void and an error issued if a temporary file could not be created.
>
> The macros `mkstemp` and `maketemp` are recognized only with parameters.

If you try this next example, you will most likely get different output for the two file names, since the replacement characters are randomly chosen:

```
$ m4
define(`tmp', `oops')
⇒
maketemp(`/tmp/fooXXXXXX')
⇒/tmp/fooa07346
ifdef(`mkstemp', `define(`maketemp', defn(`mkstemp'))',
       `define(`mkstemp', defn(`maketemp'))dnl
errprint(`warning: potentially insecure maketemp implementation
')')
⇒
mkstemp(`doc')
⇒docQv83Uw
```

Unless you use the `--traditional` command line option (or `-G`, see Section 2.3 [Invoking m4], page 10), the GNU version of `maketemp` is secure. This means that using the same template to multiple calls will generate multiple files. However, we recommend that you use the new `mkstemp` macro, introduced in GNU M4 1.4.8, which is secure even in traditional mode. Also, as of M4 1.4.11, the secure implementation quotes the resulting file name, so that you are guaranteed to know what file was created even if the random file name happens to match an existing macro. Notice that this example is careful to use `defn` to avoid unintended expansion of 'foo'.

```
$ m4
define('foo', 'errprint('oops')')
⇒
syscmd('rm -f foo-??????')sysval
⇒0
define('file1', maketemp('foo-XXXXXX'))dnl
ifelse(esyscmd('echo \' foo-?????? \''), ' foo-?????? ',
       'no file', 'created')
⇒created
define('file2', maketemp('foo-XX'))dnl
define('file3', mkstemp('foo-XXXXXX'))dnl
ifelse(len(defn('file1')), len(defn('file2')),
       'same length', 'different')
⇒same length
ifelse(defn('file1'), defn('file2'), 'same', 'different file')
⇒different file
ifelse(defn('file2'), defn('file3'), 'same', 'different file')
⇒different file
ifelse(defn('file1'), defn('file3'), 'same', 'different file')
⇒different file
syscmd('rm 'defn('file1') defn('file2') defn('file3'))
⇒
sysval
⇒0
```

14 Miscellaneous builtin macros

This chapter describes various builtins, that do not really belong in any of the previous chapters.

14.1 Printing error messages

You can print error messages using `errprint`:

`errprint (`*`message`*`, ...)`   [Builtin]

> Prints *message* and the rest of the arguments to standard error, separated by spaces. Standard error is used, regardless of the `--debugfile` option (see Section 2.5 [Invoking m4], page 11).
>
> The expansion of `errprint` is void. The macro `errprint` is recognized only with parameters.
>
> ```
> errprint('Invalid arguments to forloop
> ')
> ```
> error Invalid arguments to forloop
> ⇒
> ```
> errprint('1')errprint('2','3
> ')
> ```
> error 12 3
> ⇒

A trailing newline is *not* printed automatically, so it should be supplied as part of the argument, as in the example. Unfortunately, the exact output of `errprint` is not very portable to other `m4` implementations: POSIX requires that all arguments be printed, but some implementations of `m4` only print the first. Furthermore, some BSD implementations always append a newline for each `errprint` call, regardless of whether the last argument already had one, and POSIX is silent on whether this is acceptable.

14.2 Printing current location

To make it possible to specify the location of an error, three utility builtins exist:

`__file__`   [Builtin]
`__line__`   [Builtin]
`__program__`   [Builtin]

> Expand to the quoted name of the current input file, the current input line number in that file, and the quoted name of the current invocation of `m4`.
>
> ```
> errprint(__program__:__file__:__line__: 'input error
> ')
> ```
> error m4:stdin:1: input error
> ⇒

Line numbers start at 1 for each file. If the file was found due to the `-I` option or `M4PATH` environment variable, that is reflected in the file name. The syncline option (`-s`, see Section 2.2 [Invoking m4], page 8), and the 'f' and 'l' flags of `debugmode` (see Section 7.3

[Debug Levels], page 58), also use this notion of current file and line. Redefining the three location macros has no effect on syncline, debug, warning, or error message output.

This example reuses the file `incl.m4` mentioned earlier (see Section 9.1 [Include], page 73):

```
$ m4 -I examples
define(`foo', ``$0' called at __file__:__line__')
⇒
foo
⇒foo called at stdin:2
include(`incl.m4')
⇒Include file start
⇒foo called at examples/incl.m4:2
⇒Include file end
⇒
```

The location of macros invoked during the rescanning of macro expansion text corresponds to the location in the file where the expansion was triggered, regardless of how many newline characters the expansion text contains. As of GNU M4 1.4.8, the location of text wrapped with `m4wrap` (see Section 8.5 [M4wrap], page 70) is the point at which the `m4wrap` was invoked. Previous versions, however, behaved as though wrapped text came from line 0 of the file "".

```
define(`echo', `$@')
⇒
define(`foo', `echo(__line__
__line__)')
⇒
echo(__line__
__line__)
⇒4
⇒5
m4wrap(`foo
')
⇒
foo(errprint(__line__
__line__
))
error 8
error 9
⇒8
⇒8
__line__
⇒11
m4wrap(`__line__
')
⇒
^D
⇒12
```

⇒6
⇒6

The `__program__` macro behaves like '$0' in shell terminology. If you invoke m4 through an absolute path or a link with a different spelling, rather than by relying on a PATH search for plain 'm4', it will affect how `__program__` expands. The intent is that you can use it to produce error messages with the same formatting that m4 produces internally. It can also be used within **syscmd** (see Section 13.2 [Syscmd], page 96) to pick the same version of m4 that is currently running, rather than whatever version of m4 happens to be first in PATH. It was first introduced in GNU M4 1.4.6.

14.3 Exiting from m4

If you need to exit from m4 before the entire input has been read, you can use m4exit:

m4exit (*[code = '0']*)   [Builtin]

> Causes m4 to exit, with exit status *code*. If *code* is left out, the exit status is zero. If *code* cannot be parsed, or is outside the range of 0 to 255, the exit status is one. No further input is read, and all wrapped and diverted text is discarded.
>
> ```
> m4wrap('This text is lost due to 'm4exit'.')
> ⇒
> divert('1') So is this.
> divert
> ⇒
> m4exit And this is never read.
> ```

A common use of this is to abort processing:

fatal_error (*message*)   [Composite]

> Abort processing with an error message and non-zero status. Prefix *message* with details about where the error occurred, and print the resulting string to standard error.
>
> ```
> define('fatal_error',
>        'errprint(__program__:__file__:__line__': fatal error: $*
> ')m4exit('1')')
> ⇒
> fatal_error('this is a BAD one, buster')
> ```
> `error` m4:stdin:4: fatal error: this is a BAD one, buster

After this macro call, m4 will exit with exit status 1. This macro is only intended for error exits, since the normal exit procedures are not followed, i.e., diverted text is not undiverted, and saved text (see Section 8.5 [M4wrap], page 70) is not reread. (This macro could be made more robust to earlier versions of m4. You should try to see if you can find weaknesses and correct them; or see Section 17.8 [Answers], page 129).

Note that it is still possible for the exit status to be different than what was requested by **m4exit**. If m4 detects some other error, such as a write error on standard output, the exit status will be non-zero even if **m4exit** requested zero.

If standard input is seekable, then the file will be positioned at the next unread character. If it is a pipe or other non-seekable file, then there are no guarantees how much data m4 might have read into buffers, and thus discarded.

15 Fast loading of frozen state

Some bigger `m4` applications may be built over a common base containing hundreds of definitions and other costly initializations. Usually, the common base is kept in one or more declarative files, which files are listed on each `m4` invocation prior to the user's input file, or else each input file uses `include`.

Reading the common base of a big application, over and over again, may be time consuming. GNU `m4` offers some machinery to speed up the start of an application using lengthy common bases.

15.1 Using frozen files

Suppose a user has a library of `m4` initializations in `base.m4`, which is then used with multiple input files:

```
$ m4 base.m4 input1.m4
$ m4 base.m4 input2.m4
$ m4 base.m4 input3.m4
```

Rather than spending time parsing the fixed contents of `base.m4` every time, the user might rather execute:

```
$ m4 -F base.m4f base.m4
```

once, and further execute, as often as needed:

```
$ m4 -R base.m4f input1.m4
$ m4 -R base.m4f input2.m4
$ m4 -R base.m4f input3.m4
```

with the varying input. The first call, containing the -F option, only reads and executes file `base.m4`, defining various application macros and computing other initializations. Once the input file `base.m4` has been completely processed, GNU `m4` produces in `base.m4f` a *frozen* file, that is, a file which contains a kind of snapshot of the `m4` internal state.

Later calls, containing the -R option, are able to reload the internal state of `m4`, from `base.m4f`, *prior* to reading any other input files. This means instead of starting with a virgin copy of `m4`, input will be read after having effectively recovered the effect of a prior run. In our example, the effect is the same as if file `base.m4` has been read anew. However, this effect is achieved a lot faster.

Only one frozen file may be created or read in any one `m4` invocation. It is not possible to recover two frozen files at once. However, frozen files may be updated incrementally, through using -R and -F options simultaneously. For example, if some care is taken, the command:

```
$ m4 file1.m4 file2.m4 file3.m4 file4.m4
```

could be broken down in the following sequence, accumulating the same output:

```
$ m4 -F file1.m4f file1.m4
$ m4 -R file1.m4f -F file2.m4f file2.m4
$ m4 -R file2.m4f -F file3.m4f file3.m4
$ m4 -R file3.m4f file4.m4
```

Some care is necessary because not every effort has been made for this to work in all cases. In particular, the trace attribute of macros is not handled, nor the current setting of `changeword`. Currently, `m4wrap` and `sysval` also have problems. Also, interactions for some options of `m4`, being used in one call and not in the next, have not been fully analyzed yet. On the other end, you may be confident that stacks of `pushdef` definitions are handled correctly, as well as undefined or renamed builtins, and changed strings for quotes or comments. And future releases of GNU M4 will improve on the utility of frozen files.

When an `m4` run is to be frozen, the automatic undiversion which takes place at end of execution is inhibited. Instead, all positively numbered diversions are saved into the frozen file. The active diversion number is also transmitted.

A frozen file to be reloaded need not reside in the current directory. It is looked up the same way as an `include` file (see Section 9.2 [Search Path], page 74).

If the frozen file was generated with a newer version of `m4`, and contains directives that an older `m4` cannot parse, attempting to load the frozen file with option `-R` will cause `m4` to exit with status 63 to indicate version mismatch.

15.2 Frozen file format

Frozen files are sharable across architectures. It is safe to write a frozen file on one machine and read it on another, given that the second machine uses the same or newer version of GNU `m4`. It is conventional, but not required, to give a frozen file the suffix of `.m4f`.

These are simple (editable) text files, made up of directives, each starting with a capital letter and ending with a newline (NL). Wherever a directive is expected, the character '#' introduces a comment line; empty lines are also ignored if they are not part of an embedded string. In the following descriptions, each *len* refers to the length of the corresponding strings *str* in the next line of input. Numbers are always expressed in decimal. There are no escape characters. The directives are:

`C len1 , len2 NL str1 str2 NL`

> Uses *str1* and *str2* as the begin-comment and end-comment strings. If omitted, then '#' and NL are the comment delimiters.

`D number, len NL str NL`

> Selects diversion *number*, making it current, then copy *str* in the current diversion. *number* may be a negative number for a non-existing diversion. To merely specify an active selection, use this command with an empty *str*. With 0 as the diversion *number*, *str* will be issued on standard output at reload time. GNU `m4` will not produce the 'D' directive with non-zero length for diversion 0, but this can be done with manual edits. This directive may appear more than once for the same diversion, in which case the diversion is the concatenation of the various uses. If omitted, then diversion 0 is current.

`F len1 , len2 NL str1 str2 NL`

> Defines, through `pushdef`, a definition for *str1* expanding to the function whose builtin name is *str2*. If the builtin does not exist (for example, if the frozen file was produced by a copy of `m4` compiled with changeword support, but the version of `m4` reloading was compiled without it), the reload is silent, but any subsequent use of the definition of *str1* will result in a warning. This directive may appear more than once for the same name, and its order, along with 'T', is important. If omitted, you will have no access to any builtins.

`Q` *len1* `,` *len2* `NL` *str1* *str2* `NL`

> Uses *str1* and *str2* as the begin-quote and end-quote strings. If omitted, then '`'` and '`'` are the quote delimiters.

`T` *len1* `,` *len2* `NL` *str1* *str2* `NL`

> Defines, though **pushdef**, a definition for *str1* expanding to the text given by *str2*. This directive may appear more than once for the same name, and its order, along with 'F', is important.

`V` *number* `NL`

> Confirms the format of the file. **m4** 1.4.17 only creates and understands frozen files where *number* is 1. This directive must be the first non-comment in the file, and may not appear more than once.

16 Compatibility with other versions of m4

This chapter describes the many of the differences between this implementation of m4, and of other implementations found under UNIX, such as System V Release 4, Solaris, and BSD flavors. In particular, it lists the known differences and extensions to POSIX. However, the list is not necessarily comprehensive.

At the time of this writing, POSIX 2001 (also known as IEEE Std 1003.1-2001) is the latest standard, although a new version of POSIX is under development and includes several proposals for modifying what m4 is required to do. The requirements for m4 are shared between SUSv3 and POSIX, and can be viewed at http://www.opengroup.org/onlinepubs/000095399/utilities/m4.html.

16.1 Extensions in GNU M4

This version of m4 contains a few facilities that do not exist in System V m4. These extra facilities are all suppressed by using the -G command line option (see Section 2.3 [Invoking m4], page 10), unless overridden by other command line options.

- In the $n notation for macro arguments, n can contain several digits, while the System V m4 only accepts one digit. This allows macros in GNU m4 to take any number of arguments, and not only nine (see Section 5.2 [Arguments], page 26).

  This means that define('foo', '$11') is ambiguous between implementations. To portably choose between grabbing the first parameter and appending 1 to the expansion, or grabbing the eleventh parameter, you can do the following:

  ```
  define('a1', 'A1')
  ⇒
  dnl First argument, concatenated with 1
  define('_1', '$1')define('first1', '_1($@)1')
  ⇒
  dnl Eleventh argument, portable
  define('_9', '$9')define('eleventh', '_9(shift(shift($@)))')
  ⇒
  dnl Eleventh argument, GNU style
  define('Eleventh', '$11')
  ⇒
  first1('a', 'b', 'c', 'd', 'e', 'f', 'g', 'h', 'i', 'j', 'k')
  ⇒A1
  eleventh('a', 'b', 'c', 'd', 'e', 'f', 'g', 'h', 'i', 'j', 'k')
  ⇒k
  Eleventh('a', 'b', 'c', 'd', 'e', 'f', 'g', 'h', 'i', 'j', 'k')
  ⇒k
  ```

  Also see the argn macro (see Section 6.3 [Shift], page 41).

- The divert (see Section 10.1 [Divert], page 75) macro can manage more than 9 diversions. GNU m4 treats all positive numbers as valid diversions, rather than discarding diversions greater than 9.

- Files included with `include` and `sinclude` are sought in a user specified search path, if they are not found in the working directory. The search path is specified by the `-I` option and the `M4PATH` environment variable (see Section 9.2 [Search Path], page 74).

- Arguments to `undivert` can be non-numeric, in which case the named file will be included uninterpreted in the output (see Section 10.2 [Undivert], page 76).

- Formatted output is supported through the `format` builtin, which is modeled after the C library function `printf` (see Section 11.7 [Format], page 86).

- Searches and text substitution through basic regular expressions are supported by the `regexp` (see Section 11.3 [Regexp], page 81) and `patsubst` (see Section 11.6 [Patsubst], page 84) builtins. Some BSD implementations use extended regular expressions instead.

- The output of shell commands can be read into `m4` with `esyscmd` (see Section 13.3 [Esyscmd], page 97).

- There is indirect access to any builtin macro with `builtin` (see Section 5.8 [Builtin], page 35).

- Macros can be called indirectly through `indir` (see Section 5.7 [Indir], page 34).

- The name of the program, the current input file, and the current input line number are accessible through the builtins `__program__`, `__file__`, and `__line__` (see Section 14.2 [Location], page 101).

- The format of the output from `dumpdef` and macro tracing can be controlled with `debugmode` (see Section 7.3 [Debug Levels], page 58).

- The destination of trace and debug output can be controlled with `debugfile` (see Section 7.4 [Debug Output], page 60).

- The `maketemp` (see Section 13.5 [Mkstemp], page 99) macro behaves like `mkstemp`, creating a new file with a unique name on every invocation, rather than following the insecure behavior of replacing the trailing 'X' characters with the `m4` process id.

- POSIX only requires support for the command line options `-s`, `-D`, and `-U`, so all other options accepted by GNU M4 are extensions. See Chapter 2 [Invoking m4], page 7, for a description of these options.

  The debugging and tracing facilities in GNU `m4` are much more extensive than in most other versions of `m4`.

16.2 Facilities in System V `m4` not in GNU `m4`

The version of `m4` from System V contains a few facilities that have not been implemented in GNU `m4` yet. Additionally, POSIX requires some behaviors that GNU `m4` has not implemented yet. Relying on these behaviors is non-portable, as a future release of GNU `m4` may change.

- POSIX requires support for multiple arguments to `defn`, without any clarification on how `defn` behaves when one of the multiple arguments names a builtin. System V `m4` and some other implementations allow mixing builtins and text macros into a single macro. GNU `m4` only supports joining multiple text arguments, although a future implementation may lift this restriction to behave more like System V. The only portable way to join text macros with builtins is via helper macros and implicit concatenation of macro results.

- POSIX requires an application to exit with non-zero status if it wrote an error message to stderr. This has not yet been consistently implemented for the various builtins that are required to issue an error (such as `eval` (see Section 12.2 [Eval], page 89) when an argument cannot be parsed).

- Some traditional implementations only allow reading standard input once, but GNU m4 correctly handles multiple instances of '-' on the command line.

- POSIX requires `m4wrap` (see Section 8.5 [M4wrap], page 70) to act in FIFO (first-in, first-out) order, but GNU m4 currently uses LIFO order. Furthermore, POSIX states that only the first argument to `m4wrap` is saved for later evaluation, but GNU m4 saves and processes all arguments, with output separated by spaces.

- POSIX states that builtins that require arguments, but are called without arguments, have undefined behavior. Traditional implementations simply behave as though empty strings had been passed. For example, a‘’define‘’b would expand to `ab`. But GNU m4 ignores certain builtins if they have missing arguments, giving `adefineb` for the above example.

- Traditional implementations handle `define(‘f’,‘1’)` (see Section 5.1 [Define], page 25) by undefining the entire stack of previous definitions, and if doing `undefine(‘f’)` first. GNU m4 replaces just the top definition on the stack, as if doing `popdef(‘f’)` followed by `pushdef(‘f’,‘1’)`. POSIX allows either behavior.

- POSIX 2001 requires `syscmd` (see Section 13.2 [Syscmd], page 96) to evaluate command output for macro expansion, but this was a mistake that is anticipated to be corrected in the next version of POSIX. GNU m4 follows traditional behavior in `syscmd` where output is not rescanned, and provides the extension `esyscmd` that does scan the output.

- At one point, POSIX required `changequote(arg)` (see Section 8.2 [Changequote], page 62) to use newline as the close quote, but this was a bug, and the next version of POSIX is anticipated to state that using empty strings or just one argument is unspecified. Meanwhile, the GNU m4 behavior of treating an empty end-quote delimiter as ‘’ is not portable, as Solaris treats it as repeating the start-quote delimiter, and BSD treats it as leaving the previous end-quote delimiter unchanged. For predictable results, never call changequote with just one argument, or with empty strings for arguments.

- At one point, POSIX required `changecom(arg,)` (see Section 8.3 [Changecom], page 65) to make it impossible to end a comment, but this is a bug, and the next version of POSIX is anticipated to state that using empty strings is unspecified. Meanwhile, the GNU m4 behavior of treating an empty end-comment delimiter as newline is not portable, as BSD treats it as leaving the previous end-comment delimiter unchanged. It is also impossible in BSD implementations to disable comments, even though that is required by POSIX. For predictable results, never call changecom with empty strings for arguments.

- Most implementations of m4 give macros a higher precedence than comments when parsing, meaning that if the start delimiter given to `changecom` (see Section 8.3 [Changecom], page 65) starts with a macro name, comments are effectively disabled. POSIX does not specify what the precedence is, so this version of GNU m4 parser recognizes comments, then macros, then quoted strings.

- Traditional implementations allow argument collection, but not string and comment processing, to span file boundaries. Thus, if `a.m4` contains 'len(', and `b.m4` contains 'abc)', `m4 a.m4 b.m4` outputs '3' with traditional m4, but gives an error message that the end of file was encountered inside a macro with GNU m4. On the other hand, traditional implementations do end of file processing for files included with `include` or `sinclude` (see Section 9.1 [Include], page 73), while GNU m4 seamlessly integrates the content of those files. Thus `include('a.m4')include('b.m4')` will output '3' instead of giving an error.

- Traditional m4 treats `traceon` (see Section 7.2 [Trace], page 55) without arguments as a global variable, independent of named macro tracing. Also, once a macro is undefined, named tracing of that macro is lost. On the other hand, when GNU m4 encounters `traceon` without arguments, it turns tracing on for all existing definitions at the time, but does not trace future definitions; `traceoff` without arguments turns tracing off for all definitions regardless of whether they were also traced by name; and tracing by name, such as with `-tfoo` at the command line or `traceon('foo')` in the input, is an attribute that is preserved even if the macro is currently undefined.

  Additionally, while POSIX requires trace output, it makes no demands on the formatting of that output. Parsing trace output is not guaranteed to be reliable, even between different releases of GNU M4; however, the intent is that any future changes in trace output will only occur under the direction of additional `debugmode` flags (see Section 7.3 [Debug Levels], page 58).

- POSIX requires `eval` (see Section 12.2 [Eval], page 89) to treat all operators with the same precedence as C. However, earlier versions of GNU m4 followed the traditional behavior of other m4 implementations, where bitwise and logical negation ('~' and '!') have lower precedence than equality operators; and where equality operators ('==' and '!=') had the same precedence as relational operators (such as '<'). Use explicit parentheses to ensure proper precedence. As extensions to POSIX, GNU m4 gives well-defined semantics to operations that C leaves undefined, such as when overflow occurs, when shifting negative numbers, or when performing division by zero. POSIX also requires '=' to cause an error, but many traditional implementations allowed it as an alias for '=='.

- POSIX 2001 requires `translit` (see Section 11.5 [Translit], page 83) to treat each character of the second and third arguments literally. However, it is anticipated that the next version of POSIX will allow the GNU m4 behavior of treating '-' as a range operator.

- POSIX requires m4 to honor the locale environment variables of `LANG`, `LC_ALL`, `LC_CTYPE`, `LC_MESSAGES`, and `NLSPATH`, but this has not yet been implemented in GNU m4.

- POSIX states that only unquoted leading newlines and blanks (that is, space and tab) are ignored when collecting macro arguments. However, this appears to be a bug in POSIX, since most traditional implementations also ignore all whitespace (formfeed, carriage return, and vertical tab). GNU m4 follows tradition and ignores all leading unquoted whitespace.

- A strictly-compliant POSIX client is not allowed to use command-line arguments not specified by POSIX. However, since this version of M4 ignores `POSIXLY_CORRECT` and enables the option **--gnu** by default (see Section 2.3 [Invoking m4], page 10), a client desiring to be strictly compliant has no way to disable GNU extensions that conflict with POSIX when directly invoking the compiled **m4**. A future version of **GNU M4** will honor the environment variable **POSIXLY_CORRECT**, implicitly enabling **--traditional** if it is set, in order to allow a strictly-compliant client. In the meantime, a client needing strict POSIX compliance can use the workaround of invoking a shell script wrapper, where the wrapper then adds **--traditional** to the arguments passed to the compiled **m4**.

16.3 Other incompatibilities

There are a few other incompatibilities between this implementation of **m4**, and the System V version.

- GNU **m4** implements sync lines differently from System V **m4**, when text is being diverted. GNU **m4** outputs the sync lines when the text is being diverted, and System V **m4** when the diverted text is being brought back.

  The problem is which lines and file names should be attached to text that is being, or has been, diverted. System V **m4** regards all the diverted text as being generated by the source line containing the **undivert** call, whereas GNU **m4** regards the diverted text as being generated at the time it is diverted.

  The sync line option is used mostly when using **m4** as a front end to a compiler. If a diverted line causes a compiler error, the error messages should most probably refer to the place where the diversion was made, and not where it was inserted again.

  ```
  divert(2)2
  divert(1)1
  divert''0
  ⇒#line 3 "stdin"
  ⇒0
  ^D
  ⇒#line 2 "stdin"
  ⇒1
  ⇒#line 1 "stdin"
  ⇒2
  ```

  The current **m4** implementation has a limitation that the syncline output at the start of each diversion occurs no matter what, even if the previous diversion did not end with a newline. This goes contrary to the claim that synclines appear on a line by themselves, so this limitation may be corrected in a future version of **m4**. In the meantime, when using **-s**, it is wisest to make sure all diversions end with newline.

- GNU **m4** makes no attempt at prohibiting self-referential definitions like:

  ```
  define('x', 'x')
  ⇒
  define('x', 'x ')
  ⇒
  ```

  There is nothing inherently wrong with defining 'x' to return 'x'. The wrong thing is to expand 'x' unquoted, because that would cause an infinite rescan loop. In **m4**, one might use macros to hold strings, as we do for variables in other programming languages, further checking them with:

```
ifelse(defn('holder'), 'value', ...)
```

In cases like this one, an interdiction for a macro to hold its own name would be a useless limitation. Of course, this leaves more rope for the GNU `m4` user to hang himself! Rescanning hangs may be avoided through careful programming, a little like for endless loops in traditional programming languages.

17 Correct version of some examples

Some of the examples in this manuals are buggy or not very robust, for demonstration purposes. Improved versions of these composite macros are presented here.

17.1 Solution for exch

The exch macro (see Section 5.2 [Arguments], page 26) as presented requires clients to double quote their arguments. A nicer definition, which lets clients follow the rule of thumb of one level of quoting per level of parentheses, involves adding quotes in the definition of exch, as follows:

```
define('exch', ''$2', '$1'')
⇒
define(exch('expansion text', 'macro'))
⇒
macro
⇒expansion text
```

17.2 Solution for forloop

The forloop macro (see Section 6.4 [Forloop], page 46) as presented earlier can go into an infinite loop if given an iterator that is not parsed as a macro name. It does not do any sanity checking on its numeric bounds, and only permits decimal numbers for bounds. Here is an improved version, shipped as m4-1.4.17/examples/forloop2.m4; this version also optimizes overhead by calling four macros instead of six per iteration (excluding those in *text*), by not dereferencing the *iterator* in the helper _forloop.

```
$ m4 -d -I examples
undivert('forloop2.m4')dnl
⇒divert('-1')
⇒# forloop(var, from, to, stmt) - improved version:
⇒#   works even if VAR is not a strict macro name
⇒#   performs sanity check that FROM is larger than TO
⇒#   allows complex numerical expressions in TO and FROM
⇒define('forloop', 'ifelse(eval('($2) <= ($3)'), '1',
⇒   'pushdef('$1')_$0('$1', eval('$2'),
⇒     eval('$3'), '$4')popdef('$1')')')
⇒define('_forloop',
⇒   'define('$1', '$2')$4''ifelse('$2', '$3', '',
⇒     '$0('$1', incr('$2'), '$3', '$4')')')
⇒divert''dnl
include('forloop2.m4')
⇒
forloop('i', '2', '1', 'no iteration occurs')
⇒
forloop('', '1', '2', ' odd iterator name')
⇒ odd iterator name odd iterator name
forloop('i', '5 + 5', '0xc', ' 0x''eval(i, '16')')
```

```
⇒ 0xa 0xb 0xc
forloop('i', 'a', 'b', 'non-numeric bounds')
error m4:stdin:6: bad expression in eval (bad input): (a) <= (b)
⇒
```

One other change to notice is that the improved version used '_$0' rather than '_foreach' to invoke the helper routine. In general, this is a good practice to follow, because then the set of macros can be uniformly transformed. The following example shows a transformation that doubles the current quoting and appends a suffix '2' to each transformed macro. If foreach refers to the literal '_foreach', then foreach2 invokes _foreach instead of the intended _foreach2, and the mixing of quoting paradigms leads to an infinite recursion loop in this example.

```
$ m4 -d -L 9 -I examples
define('arg1', '$1')include('forloop2.m4')include('quote.m4')
⇒
define('double', 'define('$1'2',
  arg1(patsubst(dquote(defn('$1')), '['']', '\&\&')))')
⇒
double('forloop')double('_forloop')defn('forloop2')
⇒ifelse(eval('''($2) <= ($3)'''), ''1'',
⇒  ''pushdef(''$1'')_$0(''$1'', eval(''$2''),
⇒    eval(''$3''), ''$4'')popdef(''$1'')'')
forloop(i, 1, 5, 'ifelse(')forloop(i, 1, 5, ')')
⇒
changequote('[', ']')changequote([''], [''])
⇒
forloop2(i, 1, 5, ''ifelse('')forloop2(i, 1, 5, '')'')
⇒
changequote''include('forloop.m4')
⇒
double('forloop')double('_forloop')defn('forloop2')
⇒pushdef(''$1'', ''$2'')_forloop($@)popdef(''$1'')
forloop(i, 1, 5, 'ifelse(')forloop(i, 1, 5, ')')
⇒
changequote('[', ']')changequote([''], [''])
⇒
forloop2(i, 1, 5, ''ifelse('')forloop2(i, 1, 5, '')'')
error m4:stdin:12: recursion limit of 9 exceeded, use -L<N> to change it
```

One more optimization is still possible. Instead of repeatedly assigning a variable then invoking or dereferencing it, it is possible to pass the current iterator value as a single argument. Coupled with curry if other arguments are needed (see Section 6.7 [Composition], page 51), or with helper macros if the argument is needed in more than one place in the expansion, the output can be generated with three, rather than four, macros of overhead per iteration. Notice how the file m4-1.4.17/examples/forloop3.m4 rearranges the arguments of the helper _forloop to take two arguments that are placed around the current value. By splitting a balanced set of parantheses across multiple arguments, the helper macro can now be shared by forloop and the new forloop_arg.

```
$ m4 -I examples
include('forloop3.m4')
⇒
undivert('forloop3.m4')dnl
⇒divert('-1')
⇒# forloop_arg(from, to, macro) - invoke MACRO(value) for
⇒#    each value between FROM and TO, without define overhead
⇒define('forloop_arg', 'ifelse(eval('($1) <= ($2)'), '1',
⇒   '_forloop('$1', eval('$2'), '$3(', ')')')')
⇒# forloop(var, from, to, stmt) - refactored to share code
⇒define('forloop', 'ifelse(eval('($2) <= ($3)'), '1',
⇒   'pushdef('$1')_forloop(eval('$2'), eval('$3'),
⇒      'define('$1',', ')$4')popdef('$1')')')
⇒define('_forloop',
⇒   '$3'$1'$4''ifelse('$1', '$2', '',
⇒      '$0(incr('$1'), '$2', '$3', '$4')')')
⇒divert''dnl
forloop('i', '1', '3', ' i')
⇒ 1 2 3
define('echo', '$@')
⇒
forloop_arg('1', '3', ' echo')
⇒ 1 2 3
include('curry.m4')
⇒
forloop_arg('1', '3', 'curry('pushdef', 'a')')
⇒
a
⇒3
popdef('a')a
⇒2
popdef('a')a
⇒1
popdef('a')a
⇒a
```

Of course, it is possible to make even more improvements, such as adding an optional step argument, or allowing iteration through descending sequences. GNU Autoconf provides some of these additional bells and whistles in its `m4_for` macro.

17.3 Solution for `foreach`

The `foreach` and `foreachq` macros (see Section 6.5 [Foreach], page 47) as presented earlier each have flaws. First, we will examine and fix the quadratic behavior of `foreachq`:

```
$ m4 -I examples
include('foreachq.m4')
⇒
traceon('shift')debugmode('aq')
```

```
⇒
foreachq('x', ''1', '2', '3', '4'', 'x
')dnl
⇒1
[error] m4trace: -3- shift('1', '2', '3', '4')
[error] m4trace: -2- shift('1', '2', '3', '4')
⇒2
[error] m4trace: -4- shift('1', '2', '3', '4')
[error] m4trace: -3- shift('2', '3', '4')
[error] m4trace: -3- shift('1', '2', '3', '4')
[error] m4trace: -2- shift('2', '3', '4')
⇒3
[error] m4trace: -5- shift('1', '2', '3', '4')
[error] m4trace: -4- shift('2', '3', '4')
[error] m4trace: -3- shift('3', '4')
[error] m4trace: -4- shift('1', '2', '3', '4')
[error] m4trace: -3- shift('2', '3', '4')
[error] m4trace: -2- shift('3', '4')
⇒4
[error] m4trace: -6- shift('1', '2', '3', '4')
[error] m4trace: -5- shift('2', '3', '4')
[error] m4trace: -4- shift('3', '4')
[error] m4trace: -3- shift('4')
```

Each successive iteration was adding more quoted `shift` invocations, and the entire list contents were passing through every iteration. In general, when recursing, it is a good idea to make the recursion use fewer arguments, rather than adding additional quoted uses of `shift`. By doing so, m4 uses less memory, invokes fewer macros, is less likely to run into machine limits, and most importantly, performs faster. The fixed version of `foreachq` can be found in `m4-1.4.17/examples/foreachq2.m4`:

```
$ m4 -I examples
include('foreachq2.m4')
⇒
undivert('foreachq2.m4')dnl
⇒include('quote.m4')dnl
⇒divert('-1')
⇒# foreachq(x, 'item_1, item_2, ..., item_n', stmt)
⇒#   quoted list, improved version
⇒define('foreachq', 'pushdef('$1')_$0($@)popdef('$1')')
⇒define('_arg1q', ''$1'')
⇒define('_rest', 'ifelse('$#', '1', '', 'dquote(shift($@))')')
⇒define('_foreachq', 'ifelse('$2', '', '',
⇒  'define('$1', _arg1q($2))$3''$0('$1', _rest($2), '$3')')')
⇒divert''dnl
traceon('shift')debugmode('aq')
⇒
foreachq('x', ''1', '2', '3', '4'', 'x
```

```
')dnl
⇒1
error  m4trace: -3- shift('1', '2', '3', '4')
⇒2
error  m4trace: -3- shift('2', '3', '4')
⇒3
error  m4trace: -3- shift('3', '4')
⇒4
```

Note that the fixed version calls unquoted helper macros in _foreachq to trim elements immediately; those helper macros in turn must re-supply the layer of quotes lost in the macro invocation. Contrast the use of _arg1q, which quotes the first list element, with _arg1 of the earlier implementation that returned the first list element directly. Additionally, by calling the helper method immediately, the 'defn('iterator')' no longer contains unexpanded macros.

The astute m4 programmer might notice that the solution above still uses more memory and macro invocations, and thus more time, than strictly necessary. Note that '$2', which contains an arbitrarily long quoted list, is expanded and rescanned three times per iteration of _foreachq. Furthermore, every iteration of the algorithm effectively unboxes then reboxes the list, which costs a couple of macro invocations. It is possible to rewrite the algorithm for a bit more speed by swapping the order of the arguments to _foreachq in order to operate on an unboxed list in the first place, and by using the fixed-length '$#' instead of an arbitrary length list as the key to end recursion. The result is an overhead of six macro invocations per loop (excluding any macros in *text*), instead of eight. This alternative approach is available as m4-1.4.17/examples/foreach3.m4:

```
$ m4 -I examples
include('foreachq3.m4')
⇒
undivert('foreachq3.m4')dnl
⇒divert('-1')
⇒# foreachq(x, 'item_1, item_2, ..., item_n', stmt)
⇒#   quoted list, alternate improved version
⇒define('foreachq', 'ifelse('$2', '', '',
⇒  'pushdef('$1')_$0('$1', '$3', '', $2)popdef('$1')')')
⇒define('_foreachq', 'ifelse('$#', '3', '',
⇒  'define('$1', '$4')$2''$0('$1', '$2',
⇒    shift(shift(shift($@))))')')
⇒divert''dnl
traceon('shift')debugmode('aq')
⇒
foreachq('x', ''1', '2', '3', '4'', 'x
')dnl
⇒1
error  m4trace: -4- shift('x', 'x
error  ', '', '1', '2', '3', '4')
error  m4trace: -3- shift('x
error  ', '', '1', '2', '3', '4')
```

```
error  m4trace: -2- shift(‘’, ‘1’, ‘2’, ‘3’, ‘4’)
⇒2
error  m4trace: -4- shift(‘x’, ‘x
error  ’, ‘1’, ‘2’, ‘3’, ‘4’)
error  m4trace: -3- shift(‘x
error  ’, ‘1’, ‘2’, ‘3’, ‘4’)
error  m4trace: -2- shift(‘1’, ‘2’, ‘3’, ‘4’)
⇒3
error  m4trace: -4- shift(‘x’, ‘x
error  ’, ‘2’, ‘3’, ‘4’)
error  m4trace: -3- shift(‘x
error  ’, ‘2’, ‘3’, ‘4’)
error  m4trace: -2- shift(‘2’, ‘3’, ‘4’)
⇒4
error  m4trace: -4- shift(‘x’, ‘x
error  ’, ‘3’, ‘4’)
error  m4trace: -3- shift(‘x
error  ’, ‘3’, ‘4’)
error  m4trace: -2- shift(‘3’, ‘4’)
```

In the current version of M4, every instance of ‘$@’ is rescanned as it is encountered. Thus, the `foreachq3.m4` alternative uses much less memory than `foreachq2.m4`, and executes as much as 10% faster, since each iteration encounters fewer ‘$@’. However, the implementation of rescanning every byte in ‘$@’ is quadratic in the number of bytes scanned (for example, making the broken version in `foreachq.m4` cubic, rather than quadratic, in behavior). A future release of M4 will improve the underlying implementation by reusing results of previous scans, so that both styles of `foreachq` can become linear in the number of bytes scanned. Notice how the implementation injects an empty argument prior to expanding ‘$2’ within `foreachq`; the helper macro `_foreachq` then ignores the third argument altogether, and ends recursion when there are three arguments left because there was nothing left to pass through `shift`. Thus, each iteration only needs one `ifelse`, rather than the two conditionals used in the version from `foreachq2.m4`.

So far, all of the implementations of `foreachq` presented have been quadratic with M4 1.4.x. But `forloop` is linear, because each iteration parses a constant amount of arguments. So, it is possible to design a variant that uses `forloop` to do the iteration, then uses ‘$@’ only once at the end, giving a linear result even with older M4 implementations. This implementation relies on the GNU extension that ‘$10’ expands to the tenth argument rather than the first argument concatenated with ‘0’. The trick is to define an intermediate macro that repeats the text `m4_define(‘$1’, ‘$n’)$2‘’`, with ‘n’ set to successive integers corresponding to each argument. The helper macro `_foreachq_` is needed in order to generate the literal sequences such as ‘$1’ into the intermediate macro, rather than expanding them as the arguments of `_foreachq`. With this approach, no `shift` calls are even needed! Even though there are seven macros of overhead per iteration instead of six in `foreachq3.m4`, the linear scaling is apparent at relatively small list sizes. However, this approach will need adjustment when a future version of M4 follows POSIX by no longer treating ‘$10’ as the tenth argument; the anticipation is that ‘${10}’ can be used instead, although that alternative syntax is not yet supported.

```
$ m4 -I examples
include('foreachq4.m4')
⇒
undivert('foreachq4.m4')dnl
⇒include('forloop2.m4')dnl
⇒divert('-1')
⇒# foreachq(x, 'item_1, item_2, ..., item_n', stmt)
⇒#   quoted list, version based on forloop
⇒define('foreachq',
⇒'ifelse('$2', '', '', '_$0('$1', '$3', $2)')')
⇒define('_foreachq',
⇒'pushdef('$1', forloop('$1', '3', '$#',
⇒  '$0_('1', '2', indir('$1'))')'popdef(
⇒    '$1')')indir('$1', $@)')
⇒define('_foreachq_',
⇒''define('$$1', '$$3')$$2''')
⇒divert''dnl
traceon('shift')debugmode('aq')
⇒
foreachq('x', ''1', '2', '3', '4'', 'x
')dnl
⇒1
⇒2
⇒3
⇒4
```

For yet another approach, the improved version of foreach, available in m4-1.4.17/
examples/foreach2.m4, simply overquotes the arguments to _foreach to begin with, using
dquote_elt. Then _foreach can just use _arg1 to remove the extra layer of quoting that
was added up front:

```
$ m4 -I examples
include('foreach2.m4')
⇒
undivert('foreach2.m4')dnl
⇒include('quote.m4')dnl
⇒divert('-1')
⇒# foreach(x, (item_1, item_2, ..., item_n), stmt)
⇒#   parenthesized list, improved version
⇒define('foreach', 'pushdef('$1')_$0('$1',
⇒  (dquote(dquote_elt$2)), '$3')popdef('$1')')
⇒define('_arg1', '$1')
⇒define('_foreach', 'ifelse('$2', '('')', '',
⇒  'define('$1', _arg1$2)$3''$0('$1', (dquote(shift$2)), '$3')')')
⇒divert''dnl
traceon('shift')debugmode('aq')
⇒
foreach('x', '('1', '2', '3', '4')', 'x
```

```
')dnl
```
error m4trace: -4- shift(`1', `2', `3', `4')
error m4trace: -4- shift(`2', `3', `4')
error m4trace: -4- shift(`3', `4')
⇒1
error m4trace: -3- shift(``1'', ``2'', ``3'', ``4'')
⇒2
error m4trace: -3- shift(``2'', ``3'', ``4'')
⇒3
error m4trace: -3- shift(``3'', ``4'')
⇒4
error m4trace: -3- shift(``4'')

It is likewise possible to write a variant of foreach that performs in linear time on M4
1.4.x; the easiest method is probably writing a version of foreach that unboxes its list,
then invokes _foreachq as previously defined in foreachq4.m4.

In summary, recursion over list elements is trickier than it appeared at first glance,
but provides a powerful idiom within m4 processing. As a final demonstration, both list
styles are now able to handle several scenarios that would wreak havoc on one or both of
the original implementations. This points out one other difference between the list styles.
foreach evaluates unquoted list elements only once, in preparation for calling _foreach,
similary for foreachq as provided by foreachq3.m4 or foreachq4.m4. But foreachq, as
provided by foreachq2.m4, evaluates unquoted list elements twice while visiting the first
list element, once in _arg1q and once in _rest. When deciding which list style to use,
one must take into account whether repeating the side effects of unquoted list elements will
have any detrimental effects.

```
$ m4 -I examples
include(`foreach2.m4')
⇒
include(`foreachq2.m4')
⇒
dnl 0-element list:
foreach(`x', `', `<x>') / foreachq(`x', `', `<x>')
⇒ /
dnl 1-element list of empty element
foreach(`x', `()', `<x>') / foreachq(`x', `''', `<x>')
⇒<> / <>
dnl 2-element list of empty elements
foreach(`x', `(`',`')', `<x>') / foreachq(`x', `'',`'', `<x>')
⇒<><> / <><>
dnl 1-element list of a comma
foreach(`x', `(`,')', `<x>') / foreachq(`x', `'','', `<x>')
⇒<,> / <,>
dnl 2-element list of unbalanced parentheses
foreach(`x', `(`(', `)')', `<x>') / foreachq(`x', `'(', `)'', `<x>')
⇒<(><)> / <(><)>
define(`ab', `oops')dnl using defn(`iterator')
```

```
foreach(`x', `(`a', `b')', `defn(`x')') /dnl
 foreachq(`x', ``a', `b'', `defn(`x')')
⇒ab / ab
define(`active', `ACT, IVE')
⇒
traceon(`active')
⇒
dnl list of unquoted macros; expansion occurs before recursion
foreach(`x', `(active, active)', `<x>
')dnl
error m4trace: -4- active -> `ACT, IVE'
error m4trace: -4- active -> `ACT, IVE'
⇒<ACT>
⇒<IVE>
⇒<ACT>
⇒<IVE>
foreachq(`x', `active, active', `<x>
')dnl
error m4trace: -3- active -> `ACT, IVE'
error m4trace: -3- active -> `ACT, IVE'
⇒<ACT>
error m4trace: -3- active -> `ACT, IVE'
error m4trace: -3- active -> `ACT, IVE'
⇒<IVE>
⇒<ACT>
⇒<IVE>
dnl list of quoted macros; expansion occurs during recursion
foreach(`x', `(`active', `active')', `<x>
')dnl
error m4trace: -1- active -> `ACT, IVE'
⇒<ACT, IVE>
error m4trace: -1- active -> `ACT, IVE'
⇒<ACT, IVE>
foreachq(`x', ``active', `active'', `<x>
')dnl
error m4trace: -1- active -> `ACT, IVE'
⇒<ACT, IVE>
error m4trace: -1- active -> `ACT, IVE'
⇒<ACT, IVE>
dnl list of double-quoted macro names; no expansion
foreach(`x', `(``active'', ``active'')', `<x>
')dnl
⇒<active>
⇒<active>
foreachq(`x', ```active'', ``active''', `<x>
')dnl
⇒<active>
```

⇒<active>

17.4 Solution for copy

The macro copy presented above is unable to handle builtin tokens with M4 1.4.x, because it tries to pass the builtin token through the macro curry, where it is silently flattened to an empty string (see Section 6.7 [Composition], page 51). Rather than using the problematic curry to work around the limitation that stack_foreach expects to invoke a macro that takes exactly one argument, we can write a new macro that lets us form the exact two-argument pushdef call sequence needed, so that we are no longer passing a builtin token through a text macro.

stack_foreach_sep (*macro*, *pre*, *post*, *sep*)   [Composite]
stack_foreach_sep_lifo (*macro*, *pre*, *post*, *sep*)   [Composite]
> For each of the pushdef definitions associated with *macro*, expand the sequence 'pre''definition''post'. Additionally, expand *sep* between definitions. stack_foreach_sep visits the oldest definition first, while stack_foreach_sep_lifo visits the current definition first. The expansion may dereference *macro*, but should not modify it. There are a few special macros, such as defn, which cannot be used as the *macro* parameter.

Note that stack_foreach('*macro*', '*action*') is equivalent to stack_foreach_sep('*macro*', '*action*(', ')'). By supplying explicit parentheses, split among the *pre* and *post* arguments to stack_foreach_sep, it is now possible to construct macro calls with more than one argument, without passing builtin tokens through a macro call. It is likewise possible to directly reference the stack definitions without a macro call, by leaving *pre* and *post* empty. Thus, in addition to fixing copy on builtin tokens, it also executes with fewer macro invocations.

The new macro also adds a separator that is only output after the first iteration of the helper _stack_reverse_sep, implemented by prepending the original *sep* to *pre* and omitting a *sep* argument in subsequent iterations. Note that the empty string that separates *sep* from *pre* is provided as part of the fourth argument when originally calling _stack_reverse_sep, and not by writing $4''$3 as the third argument in the recursive call; while the other approach would give the same output, it does so at the expense of increasing the argument size on each iteration of _stack_reverse_sep, which results in quadratic instead of linear execution time. The improved stack walking macros are available in m4-1.4.17/examples/stack_sep.m4:

```
$ m4 -I examples
include('stack_sep.m4')
⇒
define('copy', 'ifdef('$2', 'errprint('$2 already defined
')m4exit('1')',
   'stack_foreach_sep('$1', 'pushdef('$2',', ')')')')')dnl
pushdef('a', '1')pushdef('a', defn('divnum'))
⇒
copy('a', 'b')
⇒
b
```

```
⇒0
popdef('b')
⇒
b
⇒1
pushdef('c', '1')pushdef('c', '2')
⇒
stack_foreach_sep_lifo('c', '', '', ', ')
⇒2, 1
undivert('stack_sep.m4')dnl
⇒divert('-1')
⇒# stack_foreach_sep(macro, pre, post, sep)
⇒# Invoke PRE''defn''POST with a single argument of each definition
⇒# from the definition stack of MACRO, starting with the oldest, and
⇒# separated by SEP between definitions.
⇒define('stack_foreach_sep',
⇒'_stack_reverse_sep('$1', 'tmp-$1')'dnl
⇒'_stack_reverse_sep('tmp-$1', '$1', '$2''defn('$1')$3', '$4''')')
⇒# stack_foreach_sep_lifo(macro, pre, post, sep)
⇒# Like stack_foreach_sep, but starting with the newest definition.
⇒define('stack_foreach_sep_lifo',
⇒'_stack_reverse_sep('$1', 'tmp-$1', '$2''defn('$1')$3', '$4''')'dnl
⇒'_stack_reverse_sep('tmp-$1', '$1')')
⇒define('_stack_reverse_sep',
⇒'ifdef('$1', 'pushdef('$2', defn('$1'))$3''popdef('$1')$0(
⇒  '$1', '$2', '$4$3')')')
⇒divert''dnl
```

17.5 Solution for m4wrap

The replacement m4wrap versions presented above, designed to guarantee FIFO or LIFO order regardless of the underlying M4 implementation, share a bug when dealing with wrapped text that looks like parameter expansion. Note how the invocation of m4wrapn interprets these parameters, while using the builtin preserves them for their intended use.

```
$ m4 -I examples
include('wraplifo.m4')
⇒
m4wrap('define('foo', ''$0:'-$1-$*-$#-')foo('a', 'b')
')
⇒
builtin('m4wrap', '''define('bar', ''$0:'-$1-$*-$#-')bar('a', 'b')
')
⇒
^D
⇒bar:-a-a,b-2-
⇒m4wrap0:---0-
```

Additionally, the computation of `_m4wrap_level` and creation of multiple `m4wrapn` place-holders in the original examples is more expensive in time and memory than strictly necessary. Notice how the improved version grabs the wrapped text via `defn` to avoid parameter expansion, then undefines `_m4wrap_text`, before stripping a level of quotes with `_arg1` to expand the text. That way, each level of wrapping reuses the single placeholder, which starts each nesting level in an undefined state.

Finally, it is worth emulating the GNU M4 extension of saving all arguments to `m4wrap`, separated by a space, rather than saving just the first argument. This is done with the `join` macro documented previously (see Section 6.3 [Shift], page 41). The improved LIFO example is shipped as `m4-1.4.17/examples/wraplifo2.m4`, and can easily be converted to a FIFO solution by swapping the adjacent invocations of `joinall` and `defn`.

```
$ m4 -I examples
include('wraplifo2.m4')
⇒
undivert('wraplifo2.m4')dnl
⇒dnl Redefine m4wrap to have LIFO semantics, improved example.
⇒include('join.m4')dnl
⇒define('_m4wrap', defn('m4wrap'))dnl
⇒define('_arg1', '$1')dnl
⇒define('m4wrap',
⇒'ifdef('_$0_text',
⇒        'define('_$0_text', joinall(' ', $@)defn('_$0_text'))',
⇒        '_$0('_arg1(defn('_$0_text')undefine('_$0_text'))')dnl
⇒define('_$0_text', joinall(' ', $@))')')dnl
m4wrap('define('foo', ''$0:'-$1-$*-$#-')foo('a', 'b')
')
⇒
m4wrap('lifo text
m4wrap('nested', '', '$@
')')
⇒
^D
⇒lifo text
⇒foo:-a-a,b-2-
⇒nested $@
```

17.6 Solution for `cleardivert`

The `cleardivert` macro (see Section 10.4 [Cleardivert], page 79) cannot, as it stands, be called without arguments to clear all pending diversions. That is because using undivert with an empty string for an argument is different than using it with no arguments at all. Compare the earlier definition with one that takes the number of arguments into account:

```
define('cleardivert',
   'pushdef('_n', divnum)divert('-1')undivert($@)divert(_n)popdef('_n')')
⇒
divert('1')one
divert
```

```
⇒
cleardivert
⇒
undivert
⇒one
⇒
define('cleardivert',
  'pushdef('_num', divnum)divert('-1')ifelse('$#', '0',
    'undivert''', 'undivert($@)')divert(_num)popdef('_num')')
⇒
divert('2')two
divert
⇒
cleardivert
⇒
undivert
⇒
```

17.7 Solution for `capitalize`

The `capitalize` macro (see Section 11.6 [Patsubst], page 84) as presented earlier does not allow clients to follow the quoting rule of thumb. Consider the three macros `active`, `Active`, and `ACTIVE`, and the difference between calling `capitalize` with the expansion of a macro, expanding the result of a case change, and changing the case of a double-quoted string:

```
$ m4 -I examples
include('capitalize.m4')dnl
define('active', 'act1, ive')dnl
define('Active', 'Act2, Ive')dnl
define('ACTIVE', 'ACT3, IVE')dnl
upcase(active)
⇒ACT1,IVE
upcase('active')
⇒ACT3, IVE
upcase(''active'')
⇒ACTIVE
downcase(ACTIVE)
⇒act3,ive
downcase('ACTIVE')
⇒act1, ive
downcase(''ACTIVE'')
⇒active
capitalize(active)
⇒Act1
capitalize('active')
⇒Active
capitalize(''active'')
```

```
⇒_capitalize('active')
define('A', 'OOPS')
⇒
capitalize(active)
⇒OOPSct1
capitalize('active')
⇒OOPSctive
```

First, when `capitalize` is called with more than one argument, it was throwing away later arguments, whereas `upcase` and `downcase` used '`$*`' to collect them all. The fix is simple: use '`$*`' consistently.

Next, with single-quoting, `capitalize` outputs a single character, a set of quotes, then the rest of the characters, making it impossible to invoke `Active` after the fact, and allowing the alternate macro `A` to interfere. Here, the solution is to use additional quoting in the helper macros, then pass the final over-quoted output string through `_arg1` to remove the extra quoting and finally invoke the concatenated portions as a single string.

Finally, when passed a double-quoted string, the nested macro `_capitalize` is never invoked because it ended up nested inside quotes. This one is the toughest to fix. In short, we have no idea how many levels of quotes are in effect on the substring being altered by `patsubst`. If the replacement string cannot be expressed entirely in terms of literal text and backslash substitutions, then we need a mechanism to guarantee that the helper macros are invoked outside of quotes. In other words, this sounds like a job for `changequote` (see Section 8.2 [Changequote], page 62). By changing the active quoting characters, we can guarantee that replacement text injected by `patsubst` always occurs in the middle of a string that has exactly one level of over-quoting using alternate quotes; so the replacement text closes the quoted string, invokes the helper macros, then reopens the quoted string. In turn, that means the replacement text has unbalanced quotes, necessitating another round of `changequote`.

In the fixed version below, (also shipped as `m4-1.4.17/examples/capitalize2.m4`), `capitalize` uses the alternate quotes of '`<<[`' and '`]>>`' (the longer strings are chosen so as to be less likely to appear in the text being converted). The helpers `_to_alt` and `_from_alt` merely reduce the number of characters required to perform a `changequote`, since the definition changes twice. The outermost pair means that `patsubst` and `_capitalize_alt` are invoked with alternate quoting; the innermost pair is used so that the third argument to `patsubst` can contain an unbalanced '`]>>`'/'`<<[`' pair. Note that `upcase` and `downcase` must be redefined as `_upcase_alt` and `_downcase_alt`, since they contain nested quotes but are invoked with the alternate quoting scheme in effect.

```
$ m4 -I examples
include('capitalize2.m4')dnl
define('active', 'act1, ive')dnl
define('Active', 'Act2, Ive')dnl
define('ACTIVE', 'ACT3, IVE')dnl
define('A', 'OOPS')dnl
capitalize(active; 'active'; ''active''; '''actIVE''')
⇒Act1,Ive; Act2, Ive; Active; 'Active'
undivert('capitalize2.m4')dnl
⇒divert('-1')
```

```
⇒# upcase(text)
⇒# downcase(text)
⇒# capitalize(text)
⇒#    change case of text, improved version
⇒define('upcase', 'translit('$*', 'a-z', 'A-Z')')
⇒define('downcase', 'translit('$*', 'A-Z', 'a-z')')
⇒define('_arg1', '$1')
⇒define('_to_alt', 'changequote('<<[', ']>>')')
⇒define('_from_alt', 'changequote(<<[']>>, <<[']>>)')
⇒define('_upcase_alt', 'translit(<<[$*]>>, <<[a-z]>>, <<[A-Z]>>)')
⇒define('_downcase_alt', 'translit(<<[$*]>>, <<[A-Z]>>, <<[a-z]>>)')
⇒define('_capitalize_alt',
⇒   'regexp(<<[$1]>>, <<[^\(\w\)\(\w*\)]>>,
⇒      <<[_upcase_alt(<<[<<[\1]>>]>>)_downcase_alt(<<[<<[\2]>>]>>)]>>)')
⇒define('capitalize',
⇒   '_arg1(_to_alt()patsubst(<<[<<[$*]>>]>>, <<[\w+]>>,
⇒      _from_alt()']>>_$0_alt(<<[\&]>>)<<[']_to_alt())_from_alt())')
⇒divert''dnl
```

17.8 Solution for `fatal_error`

The `fatal_error` macro (see Section 14.3 [M4exit], page 103) is not robust to versions of GNU M4 earlier than 1.4.8, where invoking `__file__` (see Section 14.2 [Location], page 101) inside `m4wrap` would result in an empty string, and `__line__` resulted in '0' even though all files start at line 1. Furthermore, versions earlier than 1.4.6 did not support the `__program__` macro. If you want `fatal_error` to work across the entire 1.4.x release series, a better implementation would be:

```
define('fatal_error',
  'errprint(ifdef('__program__', '__program__', ''m4'')'dnl
':ifelse(__line__, '0', '',
    '__file__:__line__:')' fatal error: $*
')m4exit('1')')
⇒
m4wrap('divnum('demo of internal message')
fatal_error('inside wrapped text')')
⇒
^D
```
error m4:stdin:6: Warning: excess arguments to builtin 'divnum' ignored
```
⇒0
```
error m4:stdin:6: fatal error: inside wrapped text

Appendix A How to make copies of the overall M4 package

This appendix covers the license for copying the source code of the overall M4 package. This manual is under a different set of restrictions, covered later (see Appendix B [Copying This Manual], page 143).

A.1 License for copying the M4 package

Version 3, 29 June 2007

Copyright © 2007 Free Software Foundation, Inc. `http://fsf.org/`

> Everyone is permitted to copy and distribute verbatim copies of this license document, but changing it is not allowed.

Preamble

The GNU General Public License is a free, copyleft license for software and other kinds of works.

The licenses for most software and other practical works are designed to take away your freedom to share and change the works. By contrast, the GNU General Public License is intended to guarantee your freedom to share and change all versions of a program—to make sure it remains free software for all its users. We, the Free Software Foundation, use the GNU General Public License for most of our software; it applies also to any other work released this way by its authors. You can apply it to your programs, too.

When we speak of free software, we are referring to freedom, not price. Our General Public Licenses are designed to make sure that you have the freedom to distribute copies of free software (and charge for them if you wish), that you receive source code or can get it if you want it, that you can change the software or use pieces of it in new free programs, and that you know you can do these things.

To protect your rights, we need to prevent others from denying you these rights or asking you to surrender the rights. Therefore, you have certain responsibilities if you distribute copies of the software, or if you modify it: responsibilities to respect the freedom of others.

For example, if you distribute copies of such a program, whether gratis or for a fee, you must pass on to the recipients the same freedoms that you received. You must make sure that they, too, receive or can get the source code. And you must show them these terms so they know their rights.

Developers that use the GNU GPL protect your rights with two steps: (1) assert copyright on the software, and (2) offer you this License giving you legal permission to copy, distribute and/or modify it.

For the developers' and authors' protection, the GPL clearly explains that there is no warranty for this free software. For both users' and authors' sake, the GPL requires that modified versions be marked as changed, so that their problems will not be attributed erroneously to authors of previous versions.

Some devices are designed to deny users access to install or run modified versions of the software inside them, although the manufacturer can do so. This is fundamentally incompatible with the aim of protecting users' freedom to change the software. The systematic pattern of such abuse occurs in the area of products for individuals to use, which is precisely where it is most unacceptable. Therefore, we have designed this version of the GPL to prohibit the practice for those products. If such problems arise substantially in other domains, we stand ready to extend this provision to those domains in future versions of the GPL, as needed to protect the freedom of users.

Finally, every program is threatened constantly by software patents. States should not allow patents to restrict development and use of software on general-purpose computers, but in those that do, we wish to avoid the special danger that patents applied to a free program could make it effectively proprietary. To prevent this, the GPL assures that patents cannot be used to render the program non-free.

The precise terms and conditions for copying, distribution and modification follow.

TERMS AND CONDITIONS

0. Definitions.

   "This License" refers to version 3 of the GNU General Public License.

   "Copyright" also means copyright-like laws that apply to other kinds of works, such as semiconductor masks.

   "The Program" refers to any copyrightable work licensed under this License. Each licensee is addressed as "you". "Licensees" and "recipients" may be individuals or organizations.

   To "modify" a work means to copy from or adapt all or part of the work in a fashion requiring copyright permission, other than the making of an exact copy. The resulting work is called a "modified version" of the earlier work or a work "based on" the earlier work.

   A "covered work" means either the unmodified Program or a work based on the Program.

   To "propagate" a work means to do anything with it that, without permission, would make you directly or secondarily liable for infringement under applicable copyright law, except executing it on a computer or modifying a private copy. Propagation includes copying, distribution (with or without modification), making available to the public, and in some countries other activities as well.

   To "convey" a work means any kind of propagation that enables other parties to make or receive copies. Mere interaction with a user through a computer network, with no transfer of a copy, is not conveying.

   An interactive user interface displays "Appropriate Legal Notices" to the extent that it includes a convenient and prominently visible feature that (1) displays an appropriate copyright notice, and (2) tells the user that there is no warranty for the work (except to the extent that warranties are provided), that licensees may convey the work under this License, and how to view a copy of this License. If the interface presents a list of user commands or options, such as a menu, a prominent item in the list meets this criterion.

1. Source Code.

   The "source code" for a work means the preferred form of the work for making modifications to it. "Object code" means any non-source form of a work.

A "Standard Interface" means an interface that either is an official standard defined by a recognized standards body, or, in the case of interfaces specified for a particular programming language, one that is widely used among developers working in that language.

The "System Libraries" of an executable work include anything, other than the work as a whole, that (a) is included in the normal form of packaging a Major Component, but which is not part of that Major Component, and (b) serves only to enable use of the work with that Major Component, or to implement a Standard Interface for which an implementation is available to the public in source code form. A "Major Component", in this context, means a major essential component (kernel, window system, and so on) of the specific operating system (if any) on which the executable work runs, or a compiler used to produce the work, or an object code interpreter used to run it.

The "Corresponding Source" for a work in object code form means all the source code needed to generate, install, and (for an executable work) run the object code and to modify the work, including scripts to control those activities. However, it does not include the work's System Libraries, or general-purpose tools or generally available free programs which are used unmodified in performing those activities but which are not part of the work. For example, Corresponding Source includes interface definition files associated with source files for the work, and the source code for shared libraries and dynamically linked subprograms that the work is specifically designed to require, such as by intimate data communication or control flow between those subprograms and other parts of the work.

The Corresponding Source need not include anything that users can regenerate automatically from other parts of the Corresponding Source.

The Corresponding Source for a work in source code form is that same work.

2. Basic Permissions.

All rights granted under this License are granted for the term of copyright on the Program, and are irrevocable provided the stated conditions are met. This License explicitly affirms your unlimited permission to run the unmodified Program. The output from running a covered work is covered by this License only if the output, given its content, constitutes a covered work. This License acknowledges your rights of fair use or other equivalent, as provided by copyright law.

You may make, run and propagate covered works that you do not convey, without conditions so long as your license otherwise remains in force. You may convey covered works to others for the sole purpose of having them make modifications exclusively for you, or provide you with facilities for running those works, provided that you comply with the terms of this License in conveying all material for which you do not control copyright. Those thus making or running the covered works for you must do so exclusively on your behalf, under your direction and control, on terms that prohibit them from making any copies of your copyrighted material outside their relationship with you.

Conveying under any other circumstances is permitted solely under the conditions stated below. Sublicensing is not allowed; section 10 makes it unnecessary.

3. Protecting Users' Legal Rights From Anti-Circumvention Law.

No covered work shall be deemed part of an effective technological measure under any applicable law fulfilling obligations under article 11 of the WIPO copyright treaty adopted on 20 December 1996, or similar laws prohibiting or restricting circumvention of such measures.

When you convey a covered work, you waive any legal power to forbid circumvention of technological measures to the extent such circumvention is effected by exercising rights under this License with respect to the covered work, and you disclaim any intention to limit operation or modification of the work as a means of enforcing, against the work's users, your or third parties' legal rights to forbid circumvention of technological measures.

4. Conveying Verbatim Copies.

You may convey verbatim copies of the Program's source code as you receive it, in any medium, provided that you conspicuously and appropriately publish on each copy an appropriate copyright notice; keep intact all notices stating that this License and any non-permissive terms added in accord with section 7 apply to the code; keep intact all notices of the absence of any warranty; and give all recipients a copy of this License along with the Program.

You may charge any price or no price for each copy that you convey, and you may offer support or warranty protection for a fee.

5. Conveying Modified Source Versions.

You may convey a work based on the Program, or the modifications to produce it from the Program, in the form of source code under the terms of section 4, provided that you also meet all of these conditions:

a. The work must carry prominent notices stating that you modified it, and giving a relevant date.

b. The work must carry prominent notices stating that it is released under this License and any conditions added under section 7. This requirement modifies the requirement in section 4 to "keep intact all notices".

c. You must license the entire work, as a whole, under this License to anyone who comes into possession of a copy. This License will therefore apply, along with any applicable section 7 additional terms, to the whole of the work, and all its parts, regardless of how they are packaged. This License gives no permission to license the work in any other way, but it does not invalidate such permission if you have separately received it.

d. If the work has interactive user interfaces, each must display Appropriate Legal Notices; however, if the Program has interactive interfaces that do not display Appropriate Legal Notices, your work need not make them do so.

A compilation of a covered work with other separate and independent works, which are not by their nature extensions of the covered work, and which are not combined with it such as to form a larger program, in or on a volume of a storage or distribution medium, is called an "aggregate" if the compilation and its resulting copyright are not used to limit the access or legal rights of the compilation's users beyond what the individual works permit. Inclusion of a covered work in an aggregate does not cause this License to apply to the other parts of the aggregate.

6. Conveying Non-Source Forms.

You may convey a covered work in object code form under the terms of sections 4 and 5, provided that you also convey the machine-readable Corresponding Source under the terms of this License, in one of these ways:

   a. Convey the object code in, or embodied in, a physical product (including a physical distribution medium), accompanied by the Corresponding Source fixed on a durable physical medium customarily used for software interchange.

   b. Convey the object code in, or embodied in, a physical product (including a physical distribution medium), accompanied by a written offer, valid for at least three years and valid for as long as you offer spare parts or customer support for that product model, to give anyone who possesses the object code either (1) a copy of the Corresponding Source for all the software in the product that is covered by this License, on a durable physical medium customarily used for software interchange, for a price no more than your reasonable cost of physically performing this conveying of source, or (2) access to copy the Corresponding Source from a network server at no charge.

   c. Convey individual copies of the object code with a copy of the written offer to provide the Corresponding Source. This alternative is allowed only occasionally and noncommercially, and only if you received the object code with such an offer, in accord with subsection 6b.

   d. Convey the object code by offering access from a designated place (gratis or for a charge), and offer equivalent access to the Corresponding Source in the same way through the same place at no further charge. You need not require recipients to copy the Corresponding Source along with the object code. If the place to copy the object code is a network server, the Corresponding Source may be on a different server (operated by you or a third party) that supports equivalent copying facilities, provided you maintain clear directions next to the object code saying where to find the Corresponding Source. Regardless of what server hosts the Corresponding Source, you remain obligated to ensure that it is available for as long as needed to satisfy these requirements.

   e. Convey the object code using peer-to-peer transmission, provided you inform other peers where the object code and Corresponding Source of the work are being offered to the general public at no charge under subsection 6d.

A separable portion of the object code, whose source code is excluded from the Corresponding Source as a System Library, need not be included in conveying the object code work.

A "User Product" is either (1) a "consumer product", which means any tangible personal property which is normally used for personal, family, or household purposes, or (2) anything designed or sold for incorporation into a dwelling. In determining whether a product is a consumer product, doubtful cases shall be resolved in favor of coverage. For a particular product received by a particular user, "normally used" refers to a typical or common use of that class of product, regardless of the status of the particular user or of the way in which the particular user actually uses, or expects or is expected to use, the product. A product is a consumer product regardless of whether the product has substantial commercial, industrial or non-consumer uses, unless such uses represent the only significant mode of use of the product.

"Installation Information" for a User Product means any methods, procedures, authorization keys, or other information required to install and execute modified versions of a covered work in that User Product from a modified version of its Corresponding Source. The information must suffice to ensure that the continued functioning of the modified object code is in no case prevented or interfered with solely because modification has been made.

If you convey an object code work under this section in, or with, or specifically for use in, a User Product, and the conveying occurs as part of a transaction in which the right of possession and use of the User Product is transferred to the recipient in perpetuity or for a fixed term (regardless of how the transaction is characterized), the Corresponding Source conveyed under this section must be accompanied by the Installation Information. But this requirement does not apply if neither you nor any third party retains the ability to install modified object code on the User Product (for example, the work has been installed in ROM).

The requirement to provide Installation Information does not include a requirement to continue to provide support service, warranty, or updates for a work that has been modified or installed by the recipient, or for the User Product in which it has been modified or installed. Access to a network may be denied when the modification itself materially and adversely affects the operation of the network or violates the rules and protocols for communication across the network.

Corresponding Source conveyed, and Installation Information provided, in accord with this section must be in a format that is publicly documented (and with an implementation available to the public in source code form), and must require no special password or key for unpacking, reading or copying.

7. Additional Terms.

"Additional permissions" are terms that supplement the terms of this License by making exceptions from one or more of its conditions. Additional permissions that are applicable to the entire Program shall be treated as though they were included in this License, to the extent that they are valid under applicable law. If additional permissions apply only to part of the Program, that part may be used separately under those permissions, but the entire Program remains governed by this License without regard to the additional permissions.

When you convey a copy of a covered work, you may at your option remove any additional permissions from that copy, or from any part of it. (Additional permissions may be written to require their own removal in certain cases when you modify the work.) You may place additional permissions on material, added by you to a covered work, for which you have or can give appropriate copyright permission.

Notwithstanding any other provision of this License, for material you add to a covered work, you may (if authorized by the copyright holders of that material) supplement the terms of this License with terms:

  a. Disclaiming warranty or limiting liability differently from the terms of sections 15 and 16 of this License; or

b. Requiring preservation of specified reasonable legal notices or author attributions in that material or in the Appropriate Legal Notices displayed by works containing it; or

c. Prohibiting misrepresentation of the origin of that material, or requiring that modified versions of such material be marked in reasonable ways as different from the original version; or

d. Limiting the use for publicity purposes of names of licensors or authors of the material; or

e. Declining to grant rights under trademark law for use of some trade names, trademarks, or service marks; or

f. Requiring indemnification of licensors and authors of that material by anyone who conveys the material (or modified versions of it) with contractual assumptions of liability to the recipient, for any liability that these contractual assumptions directly impose on those licensors and authors.

All other non-permissive additional terms are considered "further restrictions" within the meaning of section 10. If the Program as you received it, or any part of it, contains a notice stating that it is governed by this License along with a term that is a further restriction, you may remove that term. If a license document contains a further restriction but permits relicensing or conveying under this License, you may add to a covered work material governed by the terms of that license document, provided that the further restriction does not survive such relicensing or conveying.

If you add terms to a covered work in accord with this section, you must place, in the relevant source files, a statement of the additional terms that apply to those files, or a notice indicating where to find the applicable terms.

Additional terms, permissive or non-permissive, may be stated in the form of a separately written license, or stated as exceptions; the above requirements apply either way.

8. Termination.

You may not propagate or modify a covered work except as expressly provided under this License. Any attempt otherwise to propagate or modify it is void, and will automatically terminate your rights under this License (including any patent licenses granted under the third paragraph of section 11).

However, if you cease all violation of this License, then your license from a particular copyright holder is reinstated (a) provisionally, unless and until the copyright holder explicitly and finally terminates your license, and (b) permanently, if the copyright holder fails to notify you of the violation by some reasonable means prior to 60 days after the cessation.

Moreover, your license from a particular copyright holder is reinstated permanently if the copyright holder notifies you of the violation by some reasonable means, this is the first time you have received notice of violation of this License (for any work) from that copyright holder, and you cure the violation prior to 30 days after your receipt of the notice.

Termination of your rights under this section does not terminate the licenses of parties who have received copies or rights from you under this License. If your rights have been terminated and not permanently reinstated, you do not qualify to receive new licenses for the same material under section 10.

9. Acceptance Not Required for Having Copies.

You are not required to accept this License in order to receive or run a copy of the Program. Ancillary propagation of a covered work occurring solely as a consequence of using peer-to-peer transmission to receive a copy likewise does not require acceptance. However, nothing other than this License grants you permission to propagate or modify any covered work. These actions infringe copyright if you do not accept this License. Therefore, by modifying or propagating a covered work, you indicate your acceptance of this License to do so.

10. Automatic Licensing of Downstream Recipients.

Each time you convey a covered work, the recipient automatically receives a license from the original licensors, to run, modify and propagate that work, subject to this License. You are not responsible for enforcing compliance by third parties with this License.

An "entity transaction" is a transaction transferring control of an organization, or substantially all assets of one, or subdividing an organization, or merging organizations. If propagation of a covered work results from an entity transaction, each party to that transaction who receives a copy of the work also receives whatever licenses to the work the party's predecessor in interest had or could give under the previous paragraph, plus a right to possession of the Corresponding Source of the work from the predecessor in interest, if the predecessor has it or can get it with reasonable efforts.

You may not impose any further restrictions on the exercise of the rights granted or affirmed under this License. For example, you may not impose a license fee, royalty, or other charge for exercise of rights granted under this License, and you may not initiate litigation (including a cross-claim or counterclaim in a lawsuit) alleging that any patent claim is infringed by making, using, selling, offering for sale, or importing the Program or any portion of it.

11. Patents.

A "contributor" is a copyright holder who authorizes use under this License of the Program or a work on which the Program is based. The work thus licensed is called the contributor's "contributor version".

A contributor's "essential patent claims" are all patent claims owned or controlled by the contributor, whether already acquired or hereafter acquired, that would be infringed by some manner, permitted by this License, of making, using, or selling its contributor version, but do not include claims that would be infringed only as a consequence of further modification of the contributor version. For purposes of this definition, "control" includes the right to grant patent sublicenses in a manner consistent with the requirements of this License.

Each contributor grants you a non-exclusive, worldwide, royalty-free patent license under the contributor's essential patent claims, to make, use, sell, offer for sale, import and otherwise run, modify and propagate the contents of its contributor version.

In the following three paragraphs, a "patent license" is any express agreement or commitment, however denominated, not to enforce a patent (such as an express permission to practice a patent or covenant not to sue for patent infringement). To "grant" such a patent license to a party means to make such an agreement or commitment not to enforce a patent against the party.

If you convey a covered work, knowingly relying on a patent license, and the Corresponding Source of the work is not available for anyone to copy, free of charge and under the terms of this License, through a publicly available network server or other readily accessible means, then you must either (1) cause the Corresponding Source to be so available, or (2) arrange to deprive yourself of the benefit of the patent license for this particular work, or (3) arrange, in a manner consistent with the requirements of this License, to extend the patent license to downstream recipients. "Knowingly relying" means you have actual knowledge that, but for the patent license, your conveying the covered work in a country, or your recipient's use of the covered work in a country, would infringe one or more identifiable patents in that country that you have reason to believe are valid.

If, pursuant to or in connection with a single transaction or arrangement, you convey, or propagate by procuring conveyance of, a covered work, and grant a patent license to some of the parties receiving the covered work authorizing them to use, propagate, modify or convey a specific copy of the covered work, then the patent license you grant is automatically extended to all recipients of the covered work and works based on it.

A patent license is "discriminatory" if it does not include within the scope of its coverage, prohibits the exercise of, or is conditioned on the non-exercise of one or more of the rights that are specifically granted under this License. You may not convey a covered work if you are a party to an arrangement with a third party that is in the business of distributing software, under which you make payment to the third party based on the extent of your activity of conveying the work, and under which the third party grants, to any of the parties who would receive the covered work from you, a discriminatory patent license (a) in connection with copies of the covered work conveyed by you (or copies made from those copies), or (b) primarily for and in connection with specific products or compilations that contain the covered work, unless you entered into that arrangement, or that patent license was granted, prior to 28 March 2007.

Nothing in this License shall be construed as excluding or limiting any implied license or other defenses to infringement that may otherwise be available to you under applicable patent law.

12. No Surrender of Others' Freedom.

If conditions are imposed on you (whether by court order, agreement or otherwise) that contradict the conditions of this License, they do not excuse you from the conditions of this License. If you cannot convey a covered work so as to satisfy simultaneously your obligations under this License and any other pertinent obligations, then as a consequence you may not convey it at all. For example, if you agree to terms that obligate you to collect a royalty for further conveying from those to whom you convey the Program, the only way you could satisfy both those terms and this License would be to refrain entirely from conveying the Program.

13. Use with the GNU Affero General Public License.

Notwithstanding any other provision of this License, you have permission to link or combine any covered work with a work licensed under version 3 of the GNU Affero General Public License into a single combined work, and to convey the resulting work.

The terms of this License will continue to apply to the part which is the covered work, but the special requirements of the GNU Affero General Public License, section 13, concerning interaction through a network will apply to the combination as such.

14. Revised Versions of this License.

   The Free Software Foundation may publish revised and/or new versions of the GNU General Public License from time to time. Such new versions will be similar in spirit to the present version, but may differ in detail to address new problems or concerns.

   Each version is given a distinguishing version number. If the Program specifies that a certain numbered version of the GNU General Public License "or any later version" applies to it, you have the option of following the terms and conditions either of that numbered version or of any later version published by the Free Software Foundation. If the Program does not specify a version number of the GNU General Public License, you may choose any version ever published by the Free Software Foundation.

   If the Program specifies that a proxy can decide which future versions of the GNU General Public License can be used, that proxy's public statement of acceptance of a version permanently authorizes you to choose that version for the Program.

   Later license versions may give you additional or different permissions. However, no additional obligations are imposed on any author or copyright holder as a result of your choosing to follow a later version.

15. Disclaimer of Warranty.

   THERE IS NO WARRANTY FOR THE PROGRAM, TO THE EXTENT PER-MITTED BY APPLICABLE LAW. EXCEPT WHEN OTHERWISE STATED IN WRITING THE COPYRIGHT HOLDERS AND/OR OTHER PARTIES PROVIDE THE PROGRAM "AS IS" WITHOUT WARRANTY OF ANY KIND, EITHER EX-PRESSED OR IMPLIED, INCLUDING, BUT NOT LIMITED TO, THE IMPLIED WARRANTIES OF MERCHANTABILITY AND FITNESS FOR A PARTICULAR PURPOSE. THE ENTIRE RISK AS TO THE QUALITY AND PERFORMANCE OF THE PROGRAM IS WITH YOU. SHOULD THE PROGRAM PROVE DEFEC-TIVE, YOU ASSUME THE COST OF ALL NECESSARY SERVICING, REPAIR OR CORRECTION.

16. Limitation of Liability.

   IN NO EVENT UNLESS REQUIRED BY APPLICABLE LAW OR AGREED TO IN WRITING WILL ANY COPYRIGHT HOLDER, OR ANY OTHER PARTY WHO MODIFIES AND/OR CONVEYS THE PROGRAM AS PERMITTED ABOVE, BE LIABLE TO YOU FOR DAMAGES, INCLUDING ANY GENERAL, SPECIAL, IN-CIDENTAL OR CONSEQUENTIAL DAMAGES ARISING OUT OF THE USE OR INABILITY TO USE THE PROGRAM (INCLUDING BUT NOT LIMITED TO LOSS OF DATA OR DATA BEING RENDERED INACCURATE OR LOSSES SUS-TAINED BY YOU OR THIRD PARTIES OR A FAILURE OF THE PROGRAM TO OPERATE WITH ANY OTHER PROGRAMS), EVEN IF SUCH HOLDER OR OTHER PARTY HAS BEEN ADVISED OF THE POSSIBILITY OF SUCH DAM-AGES.

17. Interpretation of Sections 15 and 16.

   If the disclaimer of warranty and limitation of liability provided above cannot be given local legal effect according to their terms, reviewing courts shall apply local law that most closely approximates an absolute waiver of all civil liability in connection with the Program, unless a warranty or assumption of liability accompanies a copy of the Program in return for a fee.

END OF TERMS AND CONDITIONS

How to Apply These Terms to Your New Programs

If you develop a new program, and you want it to be of the greatest possible use to the public, the best way to achieve this is to make it free software which everyone can redistribute and change under these terms.

To do so, attach the following notices to the program. It is safest to attach them to the start of each source file to most effectively state the exclusion of warranty; and each file should have at least the "copyright" line and a pointer to where the full notice is found.

```
one line to give the program's name and a brief idea of what it does.
Copyright (C) year name of author

This program is free software: you can redistribute it and/or modify
it under the terms of the GNU General Public License as published by
the Free Software Foundation, either version 3 of the License, or (at
your option) any later version.

This program is distributed in the hope that it will be useful, but
WITHOUT ANY WARRANTY; without even the implied warranty of
MERCHANTABILITY or FITNESS FOR A PARTICULAR PURPOSE.  See the GNU
General Public License for more details.

You should have received a copy of the GNU General Public License
along with this program.  If not, see http://www.gnu.org/licenses/.
```

Also add information on how to contact you by electronic and paper mail.

If the program does terminal interaction, make it output a short notice like this when it starts in an interactive mode:

```
program Copyright (C) year name of author
This program comes with ABSOLUTELY NO WARRANTY; for details type 'show w'.
This is free software, and you are welcome to redistribute it
under certain conditions; type 'show c' for details.
```

The hypothetical commands 'show w' and 'show c' should show the appropriate parts of the General Public License. Of course, your program's commands might be different; for a GUI interface, you would use an "about box".

You should also get your employer (if you work as a programmer) or school, if any, to sign a "copyright disclaimer" for the program, if necessary. For more information on this, and how to apply and follow the GNU GPL, see http://www.gnu.org/licenses/.

The GNU General Public License does not permit incorporating your program into proprietary programs. If your program is a subroutine library, you may consider it more useful to permit linking proprietary applications with the library. If this is what you want to do, use the GNU Lesser General Public License instead of this License. But first, please read http://www.gnu.org/philosophy/why-not-lgpl.html.

Appendix B How to make copies of this manual

This appendix covers the license for copying this manual. Note that some of the longer examples in this manual are also distributed in the directory `m4-1.4.17/examples/`, where a more permissive license is in effect when copying just the examples.

B.1 License for copying this manual

Version 1.3, 3 November 2008

Copyright © 2000, 2001, 2002, 2007, 2008 Free Software Foundation, Inc.
`http://fsf.org/`

> Everyone is permitted to copy and distribute verbatim copies
> of this license document, but changing it is not allowed.

0. PREAMBLE

   The purpose of this License is to make a manual, textbook, or other functional and useful document *free* in the sense of freedom: to assure everyone the effective freedom to copy and redistribute it, with or without modifying it, either commercially or non-commercially. Secondarily, this License preserves for the author and publisher a way to get credit for their work, while not being considered responsible for modifications made by others.

   This License is a kind of "copyleft", which means that derivative works of the document must themselves be free in the same sense. It complements the GNU General Public License, which is a copyleft license designed for free software.

   We have designed this License in order to use it for manuals for free software, because free software needs free documentation: a free program should come with manuals providing the same freedoms that the software does. But this License is not limited to software manuals; it can be used for any textual work, regardless of subject matter or whether it is published as a printed book. We recommend this License principally for works whose purpose is instruction or reference.

1. APPLICABILITY AND DEFINITIONS

   This License applies to any manual or other work, in any medium, that contains a notice placed by the copyright holder saying it can be distributed under the terms of this License. Such a notice grants a world-wide, royalty-free license, unlimited in duration, to use that work under the conditions stated herein. The "Document", below, refers to any such manual or work. Any member of the public is a licensee, and is addressed as "you". You accept the license if you copy, modify or distribute the work in a way requiring permission under copyright law.

   A "Modified Version" of the Document means any work containing the Document or a portion of it, either copied verbatim, or with modifications and/or translated into another language.

   A "Secondary Section" is a named appendix or a front-matter section of the Document that deals exclusively with the relationship of the publishers or authors of the Document to the Document's overall subject (or to related matters) and contains nothing that could fall directly within that overall subject. (Thus, if the Document is in part a textbook of mathematics, a Secondary Section may not explain any mathematics.) The relationship could be a matter of historical connection with the subject or with related matters, or of legal, commercial, philosophical, ethical or political position regarding them.

The "Invariant Sections" are certain Secondary Sections whose titles are designated, as being those of Invariant Sections, in the notice that says that the Document is released under this License. If a section does not fit the above definition of Secondary then it is not allowed to be designated as Invariant. The Document may contain zero Invariant Sections. If the Document does not identify any Invariant Sections then there are none.

The "Cover Texts" are certain short passages of text that are listed, as Front-Cover Texts or Back-Cover Texts, in the notice that says that the Document is released under this License. A Front-Cover Text may be at most 5 words, and a Back-Cover Text may be at most 25 words.

A "Transparent" copy of the Document means a machine-readable copy, represented in a format whose specification is available to the general public, that is suitable for revising the document straightforwardly with generic text editors or (for images composed of pixels) generic paint programs or (for drawings) some widely available drawing editor, and that is suitable for input to text formatters or for automatic translation to a variety of formats suitable for input to text formatters. A copy made in an otherwise Transparent file format whose markup, or absence of markup, has been arranged to thwart or discourage subsequent modification by readers is not Transparent. An image format is not Transparent if used for any substantial amount of text. A copy that is not "Transparent" is called "Opaque".

Examples of suitable formats for Transparent copies include plain ASCII without markup, Texinfo input format, LaTeX input format, SGML or XML using a publicly available DTD, and standard-conforming simple HTML, PostScript or PDF designed for human modification. Examples of transparent image formats include PNG, XCF and JPG. Opaque formats include proprietary formats that can be read and edited only by proprietary word processors, SGML or XML for which the DTD and/or processing tools are not generally available, and the machine-generated HTML, PostScript or PDF produced by some word processors for output purposes only.

The "Title Page" means, for a printed book, the title page itself, plus such following pages as are needed to hold, legibly, the material this License requires to appear in the title page. For works in formats which do not have any title page as such, "Title Page" means the text near the most prominent appearance of the work's title, preceding the beginning of the body of the text.

The "publisher" means any person or entity that distributes copies of the Document to the public.

A section "Entitled XYZ" means a named subunit of the Document whose title either is precisely XYZ or contains XYZ in parentheses following text that translates XYZ in another language. (Here XYZ stands for a specific section name mentioned below, such as "Acknowledgements", "Dedications", "Endorsements", or "History".) To "Preserve the Title" of such a section when you modify the Document means that it remains a section "Entitled XYZ" according to this definition.

The Document may include Warranty Disclaimers next to the notice which states that this License applies to the Document. These Warranty Disclaimers are considered to be included by reference in this License, but only as regards disclaiming warranties: any other implication that these Warranty Disclaimers may have is void and has no effect on the meaning of this License.

2. VERBATIM COPYING

You may copy and distribute the Document in any medium, either commercially or noncommercially, provided that this License, the copyright notices, and the license notice saying this License applies to the Document are reproduced in all copies, and that you add no other conditions whatsoever to those of this License. You may not use technical measures to obstruct or control the reading or further copying of the copies you make or distribute. However, you may accept compensation in exchange for copies. If you distribute a large enough number of copies you must also follow the conditions in section 3.

You may also lend copies, under the same conditions stated above, and you may publicly display copies.

3. COPYING IN QUANTITY

If you publish printed copies (or copies in media that commonly have printed covers) of the Document, numbering more than 100, and the Document's license notice requires Cover Texts, you must enclose the copies in covers that carry, clearly and legibly, all these Cover Texts: Front-Cover Texts on the front cover, and Back-Cover Texts on the back cover. Both covers must also clearly and legibly identify you as the publisher of these copies. The front cover must present the full title with all words of the title equally prominent and visible. You may add other material on the covers in addition. Copying with changes limited to the covers, as long as they preserve the title of the Document and satisfy these conditions, can be treated as verbatim copying in other respects.

If the required texts for either cover are too voluminous to fit legibly, you should put the first ones listed (as many as fit reasonably) on the actual cover, and continue the rest onto adjacent pages.

If you publish or distribute Opaque copies of the Document numbering more than 100, you must either include a machine-readable Transparent copy along with each Opaque copy, or state in or with each Opaque copy a computer-network location from which the general network-using public has access to download using public-standard network protocols a complete Transparent copy of the Document, free of added material. If you use the latter option, you must take reasonably prudent steps, when you begin distribution of Opaque copies in quantity, to ensure that this Transparent copy will remain thus accessible at the stated location until at least one year after the last time you distribute an Opaque copy (directly or through your agents or retailers) of that edition to the public.

It is requested, but not required, that you contact the authors of the Document well before redistributing any large number of copies, to give them a chance to provide you with an updated version of the Document.

4. MODIFICATIONS

You may copy and distribute a Modified Version of the Document under the conditions of sections 2 and 3 above, provided that you release the Modified Version under precisely this License, with the Modified Version filling the role of the Document, thus licensing distribution and modification of the Modified Version to whoever possesses a copy of it. In addition, you must do these things in the Modified Version:

A. Use in the Title Page (and on the covers, if any) a title distinct from that of the Document, and from those of previous versions (which should, if there were any, be listed in the History section of the Document). You may use the same title as a previous version if the original publisher of that version gives permission.

B. List on the Title Page, as authors, one or more persons or entities responsible for authorship of the modifications in the Modified Version, together with at least five of the principal authors of the Document (all of its principal authors, if it has fewer than five), unless they release you from this requirement.

C. State on the Title page the name of the publisher of the Modified Version, as the publisher.

D. Preserve all the copyright notices of the Document.

E. Add an appropriate copyright notice for your modifications adjacent to the other copyright notices.

F. Include, immediately after the copyright notices, a license notice giving the public permission to use the Modified Version under the terms of this License, in the form shown in the Addendum below.

G. Preserve in that license notice the full lists of Invariant Sections and required Cover Texts given in the Document's license notice.

H. Include an unaltered copy of this License.

I. Preserve the section Entitled "History", Preserve its Title, and add to it an item stating at least the title, year, new authors, and publisher of the Modified Version as given on the Title Page. If there is no section Entitled "History" in the Document, create one stating the title, year, authors, and publisher of the Document as given on its Title Page, then add an item describing the Modified Version as stated in the previous sentence.

J. Preserve the network location, if any, given in the Document for public access to a Transparent copy of the Document, and likewise the network locations given in the Document for previous versions it was based on. These may be placed in the "History" section. You may omit a network location for a work that was published at least four years before the Document itself, or if the original publisher of the version it refers to gives permission.

K. For any section Entitled "Acknowledgements" or "Dedications", Preserve the Title of the section, and preserve in the section all the substance and tone of each of the contributor acknowledgements and/or dedications given therein.

L. Preserve all the Invariant Sections of the Document, unaltered in their text and in their titles. Section numbers or the equivalent are not considered part of the section titles.

M. Delete any section Entitled "Endorsements". Such a section may not be included in the Modified Version.

N. Do not retitle any existing section to be Entitled "Endorsements" or to conflict in title with any Invariant Section.

O. Preserve any Warranty Disclaimers.

If the Modified Version includes new front-matter sections or appendices that qualify as Secondary Sections and contain no material copied from the Document, you may at your option designate some or all of these sections as invariant. To do this, add their titles to the list of Invariant Sections in the Modified Version's license notice. These titles must be distinct from any other section titles.

You may add a section Entitled "Endorsements", provided it contains nothing but endorsements of your Modified Version by various parties—for example, statements of peer review or that the text has been approved by an organization as the authoritative definition of a standard.

You may add a passage of up to five words as a Front-Cover Text, and a passage of up to 25 words as a Back-Cover Text, to the end of the list of Cover Texts in the Modified Version. Only one passage of Front-Cover Text and one of Back-Cover Text may be added by (or through arrangements made by) any one entity. If the Document already includes a cover text for the same cover, previously added by you or by arrangement made by the same entity you are acting on behalf of, you may not add another; but you may replace the old one, on explicit permission from the previous publisher that added the old one.

The author(s) and publisher(s) of the Document do not by this License give permission to use their names for publicity for or to assert or imply endorsement of any Modified Version.

5. COMBINING DOCUMENTS

You may combine the Document with other documents released under this License, under the terms defined in section 4 above for modified versions, provided that you include in the combination all of the Invariant Sections of all of the original documents, unmodified, and list them all as Invariant Sections of your combined work in its license notice, and that you preserve all their Warranty Disclaimers.

The combined work need only contain one copy of this License, and multiple identical Invariant Sections may be replaced with a single copy. If there are multiple Invariant Sections with the same name but different contents, make the title of each such section unique by adding at the end of it, in parentheses, the name of the original author or publisher of that section if known, or else a unique number. Make the same adjustment to the section titles in the list of Invariant Sections in the license notice of the combined work.

In the combination, you must combine any sections Entitled "History" in the various original documents, forming one section Entitled "History"; likewise combine any sections Entitled "Acknowledgements", and any sections Entitled "Dedications". You must delete all sections Entitled "Endorsements."

6. COLLECTIONS OF DOCUMENTS

You may make a collection consisting of the Document and other documents released under this License, and replace the individual copies of this License in the various documents with a single copy that is included in the collection, provided that you follow the rules of this License for verbatim copying of each of the documents in all other respects.

You may extract a single document from such a collection, and distribute it individually under this License, provided you insert a copy of this License into the extracted document, and follow this License in all other respects regarding verbatim copying of that document.

7. AGGREGATION WITH INDEPENDENT WORKS

A compilation of the Document or its derivatives with other separate and independent documents or works, in or on a volume of a storage or distribution medium, is called an "aggregate" if the copyright resulting from the compilation is not used to limit the legal rights of the compilation's users beyond what the individual works permit. When the Document is included in an aggregate, this License does not apply to the other works in the aggregate which are not themselves derivative works of the Document.

If the Cover Text requirement of section 3 is applicable to these copies of the Document, then if the Document is less than one half of the entire aggregate, the Document's Cover Texts may be placed on covers that bracket the Document within the aggregate, or the electronic equivalent of covers if the Document is in electronic form. Otherwise they must appear on printed covers that bracket the whole aggregate.

8. TRANSLATION

Translation is considered a kind of modification, so you may distribute translations of the Document under the terms of section 4. Replacing Invariant Sections with translations requires special permission from their copyright holders, but you may include translations of some or all Invariant Sections in addition to the original versions of these Invariant Sections. You may include a translation of this License, and all the license notices in the Document, and any Warranty Disclaimers, provided that you also include the original English version of this License and the original versions of those notices and disclaimers. In case of a disagreement between the translation and the original version of this License or a notice or disclaimer, the original version will prevail.

If a section in the Document is Entitled "Acknowledgements", "Dedications", or "History", the requirement (section 4) to Preserve its Title (section 1) will typically require changing the actual title.

9. TERMINATION

You may not copy, modify, sublicense, or distribute the Document except as expressly provided under this License. Any attempt otherwise to copy, modify, sublicense, or distribute it is void, and will automatically terminate your rights under this License.

However, if you cease all violation of this License, then your license from a particular copyright holder is reinstated (a) provisionally, unless and until the copyright holder explicitly and finally terminates your license, and (b) permanently, if the copyright holder fails to notify you of the violation by some reasonable means prior to 60 days after the cessation.

Moreover, your license from a particular copyright holder is reinstated permanently if the copyright holder notifies you of the violation by some reasonable means, this is the first time you have received notice of violation of this License (for any work) from that copyright holder, and you cure the violation prior to 30 days after your receipt of the notice.

Termination of your rights under this section does not terminate the licenses of parties who have received copies or rights from you under this License. If your rights have been terminated and not permanently reinstated, receipt of a copy of some or all of the same material does not give you any rights to use it.

10. FUTURE REVISIONS OF THIS LICENSE

The Free Software Foundation may publish new, revised versions of the GNU Free Documentation License from time to time. Such new versions will be similar in spirit to the present version, but may differ in detail to address new problems or concerns. See http://www.gnu.org/copyleft/.

Each version of the License is given a distinguishing version number. If the Document specifies that a particular numbered version of this License "or any later version" applies to it, you have the option of following the terms and conditions either of that specified version or of any later version that has been published (not as a draft) by the Free Software Foundation. If the Document does not specify a version number of this License, you may choose any version ever published (not as a draft) by the Free Software Foundation. If the Document specifies that a proxy can decide which future versions of this License can be used, that proxy's public statement of acceptance of a version permanently authorizes you to choose that version for the Document.

11. RELICENSING

"Massive Multiauthor Collaboration Site" (or "MMC Site") means any World Wide Web server that publishes copyrightable works and also provides prominent facilities for anybody to edit those works. A public wiki that anybody can edit is an example of such a server. A "Massive Multiauthor Collaboration" (or "MMC") contained in the site means any set of copyrightable works thus published on the MMC site.

"CC-BY-SA" means the Creative Commons Attribution-Share Alike 3.0 license published by Creative Commons Corporation, a not-for-profit corporation with a principal place of business in San Francisco, California, as well as future copyleft versions of that license published by that same organization.

"Incorporate" means to publish or republish a Document, in whole or in part, as part of another Document.

An MMC is "eligible for relicensing" if it is licensed under this License, and if all works that were first published under this License somewhere other than this MMC, and subsequently incorporated in whole or in part into the MMC, (1) had no cover texts or invariant sections, and (2) were thus incorporated prior to November 1, 2008.

The operator of an MMC Site may republish an MMC contained in the site under CC-BY-SA on the same site at any time before August 1, 2009, provided the MMC is eligible for relicensing.

ADDENDUM: How to use this License for your documents

To use this License in a document you have written, include a copy of the License in the
document and put the following copyright and license notices just after the title page:

```
Copyright (C)  year  your name.
Permission is granted to copy, distribute and/or modify this document
under the terms of the GNU Free Documentation License, Version 1.3
or any later version published by the Free Software Foundation;
with no Invariant Sections, no Front-Cover Texts, and no Back-Cover
Texts.  A copy of the license is included in the section entitled ''GNU
Free Documentation License''.
```

If you have Invariant Sections, Front-Cover Texts and Back-Cover Texts, replace the
"with...Texts." line with this:

```
with the Invariant Sections being list their titles, with
the Front-Cover Texts being list, and with the Back-Cover Texts
being list.
```

If you have Invariant Sections without Cover Texts, or some other combination of the
three, merge those two alternatives to suit the situation.

If your document contains nontrivial examples of program code, we recommend releasing
these examples in parallel under your choice of free software license, such as the GNU
General Public License, to permit their use in free software.

Appendix C Indices of concepts and macros

C.1 Index for all `m4` macros

This index covers all `m4` builtins, as well as several useful composite macros. References are exclusively to the places where a macro is introduced the first time.

C.2 Index for many concepts

www.ingramcontent.com/pod-product-compliance
Lightning Source LLC
LaVergne TN
LVHW060142070326
832902LV00018B/2911